BARD GAMES

BARD

The Shakespeare Quiz Book

Victor L. Cahn

Illustrations by David Smith

GAMES

TAYLOR TRADE PUBLISHING
Lanham • New York • Boulder • Toronto • Plymouth, UK

Published by Taylor Trade Publishing
An imprint of The Rowman & Littlefield Publishing Group, Inc.
4501 Forbes Boulevard, Suite 200, Lanham, Maryland 20706
www.rlpgtrade.com

Estover Road, Plymouth PL6 7PY, United Kingdom

Distributed by NATIONAL BOOK NETWORK

Library of Congress Cataloging-in-Publication Data
Cahn, Victor L.
  Bard Games : the Shakespeare quiz book / Victor L. Cahn ; illustrations
by David Smith.
    p. cm.
  ISBN 978-1-58979-617-1 (pbk. : alk. paper) —
  ISBN 978-1-58979-618-8 (electronic)
  1. Shakespeare, William, 1564–1616—Examinations, questions, etc.
I. Title.
  PR2987.C27 2011
  822.3'3—dc22

                                                        2011012381

Printed in the United States of America

CONTENTS

INTRODUCTION

The universal popularity of Shakespeare remains a phenomenon. Every day, in every state of our country, as well as in innumerable locales around the world, productions of his plays arc under way. Across the globe (no pun intended), Shakespeare festivals flourish. At virtually every college and university, at least one course is devoted exclusively to Shakespeare's works. In tens of thousands of secondary schools, where English curricula encompass vastly disparate novels, stories, and plays, the one constant is Shakespeare. For actors, directors, and designers, the scripts represent the ultimate challenge and constantly inspire fresh perspectives and interpretations. For scholars, critics, and, most of all, audiences, the plays are a source of unending delight.

With these thoughts in mind, I present *Bard Games: The Shakespeare Quiz Book*, a light-hearted volume that I hope will enhance readers' appreciation of the plays. Toward that end, rather than simply compiling questions and answers, I've let the teacher in me take over to offer select commentary. But don't worry: this material is brief. After all, the fun is supposed to come from the quizzes themselves.

A few words about these games. Their range of difficulty varies, for in each I've tried to include questions that might be answered by the relatively inexperienced reader, as well as some that should challenge a devoted Bardologist. Certain quizzes near the end of the book are especially challenging. Where I offer quotations for identification, the task usually involves matching them to one of the selected speakers or plays, but those who wish to make the competition more demanding can ignore such aid and thereby show off for themselves or other contestants.

My text is *The Riverside Shakespeare*, second edition (Houghton Mifflin). If minor contradictions arise with other texts, please don't blame the quizmaster. Instead, "Let's make the best of it" (*Coriolanus*, V, vi, 146).

Finally, I note that this book contains fifty-two quizzes. Why fifty-two? There's question #1. The explanation may be found on the first page of the answer section at the end of the book.

Have a good time.

QUIZZES

QUIZ #1
OPENING LINES

Where better to start than at the beginning? In Shakespeare's plays, the action moves quickly, and even first lines propel the plot and establish themes. Match each passage to the play it opens.

1. "Who's there?"
2. "So shaken as we are, so wan with care,
   Find we a time for frighted peace to pant . . ."
3. "In sooth, I know not why I am so sad . . ."
4. "Hung be the heavens with black, yield day to night!"
5. "Nay, but this dotage of our general's
   O'erflows the measure . . ."
6. "O for a Muse of fire that would ascend
   The brightest heaven of invention!"
7. "Noble patricians, patrons of my right,
   Defend the justice of my cause with arms . . ."
8. "If music be the food of love, play on . . ."
9. "You do not meet a man but frowns . . ."

a. *Henry IV, Part 1*
b. *The Comedy of Errors*
c. *Antony and Cleopatra*
d. *Hamlet*
e. *Henry VI, Part 1*
f. *The Tempest*
g. *Henry V*
h. *The Merchant of Venice*
i. *Julius Caesar*

10. "Let fame, that all hunt after in their lives, Live regist'red upon our brazen tombs . . ."

j. *All's Well That Ends Well*

11. "Proceed, Solinus, to procure my fall, And by the doom of death end woes and all."

k. *Titus Andronicus*

12. "I come no more to make you laugh . . ."

l. *Twelfth Night*

13. "Hence! home you idle creatures, get you home!"

m. *Henry VIII*

14. "Boatswain!"
15. "In delivering my son from me, I bury a second husband."

n. *Love's Labor's Lost*
o. *Cymbeline*

QUIZ #2
SETTINGS

Many of Shakespeare's stories are set in intriguing locales. Match the place at left to the appropriate play.

1. Ephesus
2. Venice, Cyprus
3. Illyria
4. Navarre
5. Padua
6. Britain, Italy
7. England, Wales
8. Vienna
9. Verona, Mantua
10. Forest of Arden

a. *As You Like It*
b. *The Winter's Tale*
c. *Much Ado About Nothing*
d. *The Comedy of Errors*
e. *Julius Caesar*
f. *Othello*
g. *Romeo and Juliet*
h. *All's Well That Ends Well*
i. *Coriolanus*
j. *The Taming of the Shrew*

11. Rossillion, Paris, Florence, Marseilles
12. Rome, Sardis, Philippi
13. Rome, Corioles, Antium
14. Sicilia, Bohemia
15. Messina

k. *Love's Labor's Lost*
l. *Twelfth Night*
m. *Measure for Measure*
n. *Cymbeline*
o. *Henry IV, Part 1*

QUIZ #3
NAME THAT PLAY (I)

Here are twenty pairs of characters. Name the play to which each pair belongs.

1. Montjoy, Hostess
2. Gratiano, Montano
3. Lavatch, Diana
4. Hubert de Burgh, Blanch
5. Sir James Tyrrel, Sir William Catesby
6. Mistress Quickly, Sir Hugh Evans
7. Gonzalo, Ceres
8. Dumaine, Dull
9. Dick the Butcher, Roger Bolingbrook
10. Chiron, Valentine
11. Dennis, William
12. Curan, Doctor
13. Curtis, Haberdasher
14. Moth, Snug
15. Fang, Snare
16. Clitus, Strato
17. Dorcas, Dion
18. Sir Henry Green, Lord Berkeley
19. Griffith, Patience
20. Pompey, Elbow

QUIZ #4
WHO'S WHO (I)

Here are brief descriptions of fifteen characters. Identify them.

1. This Greek warrior is fierce, but thick. He is about to fight his greatest opponent, when the latter claims to be a cousin, and combat is suspended.
2. This man is the confederate of a king; indeed, he probably murdered at that king's behest. Yet at a crucial moment, the same king exiles this ally for life.
3. This man is duped by someone who manipulates everyone else. He is in love with a wonderful woman, but feels scorned when she marries a general from another land.
4. This man, a military hero, meets a countess who intends to trap him, but he reverses the situation. Later his son dies in war.
5. This man counsels his children to avoid trouble by staying honest, but his own deceptions lead to his murder.
6. This man cynically reports on a political ceremony, then helps murder the greatest man of his time.
7. While this woman mourns the death of her brother, she falls in love with a young woman disguised as a young man, then marries a young man who looks like the young woman.
8. This woman is left unprotected by her husband, who worries about the state of his country. Along with her children, she is killed.
9. This man, charged with enforcing the law, finds himself vulnerable to the same instincts he decries in others.
10. This man becomes so infatuated with a woman that he betrays his best friend, then nearly rapes the object of his affection.
11. This disguised nobleman argues with a servant, then is put in the stocks.

12. With his dying words, this king prays that his murderer be forgiven.
13. This girl is the heroine of a play in which she is the only female character.
14. While this man hides behind a curtain, he hears a marriage being arranged.
15. This woman drops dead after she is kissed by another woman.

QUIZ #5
ROMEO AND JULIET

For many students and theatergoers, their introduction to Shakespeare has been the world's most famous story of young love. Try to answer these questions about the play.

1. How long does the Chorus announce that the play will last?
2. What punishment does Prince Escalus threaten in the event of further civil disorder?
3. What age does Capulet assign his daughter?
4. How does Romeo learn that Rosaline will attend the Capulet party?
5. Whom does the Nurse describe as "a man of wax"?
6. Precisely who is Queen Mab?
7. How does Tybalt recognize Romeo at the ball?
8. What line follows Juliet's sigh, "O Romeo, Romeo, wherefore art thou Romeo?"
9. By what nickname does Mercutio refer to Tybalt?
10. Who refers to himself as "fortune's fool"? And when?
11. What token does the Nurse give Romeo?
12. Before Juliet downs the drink, what does she imagine?

13. Who is supposed to deliver Friar Laurence's letter to Romeo?
14. After Juliet discovers Romeo's body, where does Friar Laurence suggest she retreat?
15. What tribute to the dead Juliet does Montague offer?

QUIZ #6
ADAPTATIONS, MUSICAL AND OTHERWISE

Shakespeare's plays have inspired all sorts of literary, musical, and theatrical creations, including countless musical and dramatic adaptations. Here are some fitting questions.

1. Richard Rodgers and Lorenz Hart, using a "book" by George Abbott, created a musical comedy based on *The Comedy of Errors*. Name the show.
2. Ten years later, Cole Porter fashioned *Kiss Me, Kate* after *The Taming of the Shrew*. What patter song is a tribute to the original playwright? And what two characters sing it?
3. As everyone knows, *West Side Story* is an updated retelling of *Romeo and Juliet*. Leonard Bernstein wrote the music, but who wrote the lyrics? And whose remarkable direction and choreography earned plaudits?
4. In 1968, the rock musical *Your Own Thing* was an Off-Broadway hit. From what play was it adapted?
5. The final two operas by this nineteenth-century Italian composer, both based on plays of Shakespeare, were among his most successful works. Name the composer and the two operas.
6. This German composer created incidental music for one of Shakespeare's comedies. He wrote the overture when

he was seventeen, then the rest of the score more than a decade later. Name the composer and the play.

7. That same play became the basis for an opera by Carl Maria von Weber. Name the opera.

8. Ralph Vaughan Williams wrote an opera after Shakespeare's *The Merry Wives of Windsor*. What is the title of the opera?

9. Berlioz, Tchaikovsky, Prokofiev, and Gounod all created works based on one of Shakespeare's plays. Name the play.

10. *Das Liebesverbot* (1835–1836), roughly "Forbidden Love," is an early work by a composer who would later change the entire nature of opera. Name the composer and the play upon which this effort is based.

11. What twentieth-century composer wrote a symphonic study called *Falstaff*?

12. Who wrote the *Coriolan* Overture?

13. What contemporary playwright wrote an even more violent version of *King Lear*?

14. What contemporary absurdist playwright created his own version of *Macbeth*?

15. In Tom Stoppard's *Rosencrantz and Guildenstern Are Dead*, what activity occupies the wandering pair at the start of the play? And why are they unnerved by it?

16. The life of Hamlet's mother, Gertrude, is the subject of a novel by what eminent American novelist?

17. This Pulitzer Prize–winning dramatist wrote a version of *Othello* called *Desdemona: A Play About a Handkerchief*, in which the only characters are three women. Name the playwright.

18. Lee Blessing wrote his version of *Hamlet* from the point of view of one minor character. Name the play.

19. In 1966, Samuel Barber's opera based on characters from one of Shakespeare's plays opened the new Metropolitan Opera at Lincoln Center. Name the opera.

20. This British playwright wrote his own version of *The Merchant of Venice* called simply *The Merchant*. Name the playwright.

QUIZ #7
SOLILOQUIES (I)

Some of the most revelatory moments in Shakespeare's plays occur when characters speak directly to the audience. Here are brief excerpts from ten famous soliloquies. Speakers' names are provided for matching purposes, but you really shouldn't need this assistance.

1. "Thou art the ruins of the noblest man
   That ever lived in the tide of times."

2. "I'll so offend, to make offense a skill,
   Redeeming time when men think least I
   will."

3. "Thus have I politicly begun my reign,
   And 'tis my hope to end successfully."

4. "Am I a coward?
   Who calls me villain, breaks my pate
   across,
   Plucks off my beard and blows it in my
   face . . ."

5. "Come, civil night,
   Thou sober-suited matron all in black,
   And learn me how to lose a winning
   match,
   Play'd for a pair of stainless maidenhoods
   . . ."

6. "Thou, Nature, art my goddess, to thy
   law
   My services are bound."

7. "We must bear all. O hard condition,
   Twin-born with greatness, subject to the
   breath
   Of every fool whose sense no more can
   feel
   But his own wringing!"

a. Viola

b. Hamlet

c. Antony

d. Richard II

e. Edmund

f. Hal

g. Juliet

8. "Disguise, I see thou art a wickedness   h. Henry V
   Wherein the pregnant enemy does much.
   How easy is it for the proper-false
   In women's waxen hearts to set their
      forms!"
9. "He's here in double trust . . ."   i. Petruchio
10. "How sweet sour music is   j. Macbeth
    When time is broke, and no proportion
       kept!"

QUIZ #8
DISGUISES

Disguises are a staple of Shakespeare's theater. One reason is
thematic: many of the plays dramatize how often appearance
contrasts with reality. Another reason is practical: women's parts
were played by boys, so masking these characters as men was
convenient. Not surprisingly, these disguises are virtually always
undetected. Here are descriptions of fifteen characters who
adopt a different persona. Identify each character.

1. This woman carries love-messages from the man she loves
   to the woman he loves.
2. As a friar, this man secretly surveys the lawlessness rampant
   in his city.
3. She pursues a man who betrays his best friend in order to
   win that friend's lady love.
4. This woman accompanies her cousin into the forest and is
   later betrothed to a reformed villain.
5. This servant stands by his master through trials and storms.
6. This woman joins with cohorts in the guise of peasants to
   rout their nation's enemy.

7. This woman masks herself as a pilgrim to pursue the standoffish fellow for whom she longs.
8. These men dress up as foreigners to fool the ladies they love, but the trick only creates greater confusion.
9. This woman appears as Revenge before the door of her sworn enemy.
10. This woman takes to the woods both to escape her stepmother and to find the man she loves.
11. This woman saves her husband's best friend from gruesome punishment.
12. To win the woman of his dreams, this fellow disguises himself as his own servant.
13. This desperate man disguises himself to learn the truth about his wife's infidelity.
14. This woman disguises herself to marry her own husband.
15. This leader disguises himself to learn the true feelings of his soldiers.

QUIZ #9
THE STAGE ITSELF

"All the world's a stage," says Jaques in *As You Like It*. As a man of the theater, Shakespeare was fond of references to his profession. Here are a few. Match them to the speaker.

1. "Our revels now are ended. These our actors
   (As I foretold you) were all spirits and
   Are melted into air, into thin air . . ."

   a. Cassius

2. "Life's but a walking shadow, a poor player,
   That struts and frets his hour upon the stage,
   And then is heard no more."

   b. Theseus

3. "When we are born, we cry that we are come
   To this great stage of fools."

   c. York

4. "I hold the world but as the world . . .
   A stage, where every man must play a part,
   And mine a sad one."

   d. Prospero

5. "Saucy lictors
   Will catch at us like strumpets, and scald rhymers
   Ballad 's out a' tune. The quick comedians
   Extemporally will stage us . . ."

   e. King Lear

6. "As in a theater the eyes of men,
   After a well-graced actor leaves the stage,
   Are idly bent on him that enters next . . ."

   f. Macbeth

7. "And like a strutting player, whose conceit
   Lies in his hamstring, and doth think it rich
   To hear the wooden dialogue and sound . . ."

   g. Cleopatra

8. "No epilogue, I pray you; for your play needs no excuse."

   h. Ulysses

9. "Suit the action to the word, the word to the action, with this special observance, that you o'erstep not the modesty of nature . . ."

   i. Antonio

10. "How many ages hence
    Shall this our lofty scene be acted over
    In states unborn and accents yet unknown!"

    j. Hamlet

QUIZ #10
THE TAMING OF THE SHREW

Here are some tidbits about the quintessential (and controversial) battle of the sexes.

1. What is Christopher Sly's occupation?
2. Whom do the revelers dress as a lady?
3. What explanation does Petruchio give for his coming to Padua?
4. What is the family name of Baptista, Bianca, and Katherina?
5. When Tranio urges Petruchio to "break the ice," to what is Tranio referring?
6. What name does the disguised Hortensio take?
7. Who is Cambio?
8. Why does Katherina break a lute over Hortensio's head?
9. Which of Bianca's suitors is an old man?
10. Who describes Petruchio's wedding outfit?
11. When does Petruchio remind Katherina, "For 'tis the mind that makes the body rich"?
12. Identify the speaker: "By this reck'ning, he is more shrew than she."
13. Identify the speaker: "This is a way to kill a wife with kindness."
14. Whom does Katherina describe as "Young budding virgin, fair and fresh"?
15. To what does Katherina compare the duty "a woman oweth to her husband"?

QUIZ #11
WHO'S WHO (II)

Here are more descriptions, these of characters not quite so prominent.

1. This man tries to serve as comic relief but is no match for the glorious lecher and thief whose place he's trying to take.

2. This man is elected ruler but is frustrated when he loses the young woman he seeks to marry. He is killed by a son of the man he kills.

3. This simple farm girl is pursued, after a fashion, by a snooty fellow from court. After she fails to grasp most of his disparagement, they marry.

4. This boisterous fellow claims to play "the clown," but when several of his friends end up in legal difficulty, he is surprisingly vicious toward the plaintiff.

5. This man does little but rail on the foolishness of war, its leaders, and their sexual aggression. When challenged, he retreats under the excuse that he is a bastard.

6. This man offers to marry a woman who has been first disinherited by her father, then rejected by another suitor.

7. This man dies in the Tower of London, believing himself to be the victim of one of his brothers when in fact he is the victim of another brother who orders him to be murdered.

8. This man raises two of the King's children as his own.

9. This man is a mercenary who under capture reveals his own cowardice.

10. This man usurped his brother's throne. Although that throne is eventually restored, this man shows no sign of remorse or reform.

11. This person tries to arrange a marriage to promote an alliance.

12. This man finds a rebel in a garden, kills that rebel, and is knighted.

13. This Irish soldier bands together with warriors of other nations to demonstrate loyalty toward one great ruler.

14. This draftee shows a willingness to fight for a cause he really doesn't understand.

15. This man writes a sonnet to his horse.

QUIZ #12
INSULTS

No writer has ever used vituperative language more effectively than Shakespeare. Here are fifteen examples of his skill at this underappreciated art. Match the insults to the speaker and the target.

1. "Thou liest, malignant thing!"
2. "Get you gone, you dwarf; You minimus, of hind'ring knot-grass made; You bead, you acorn."
3. "You common cry of curs, whose breath I hate As reek a' th' rotten fens, whose loves I prize As the dead carcasses of unburied men . . ."
4. "Why, thou clay-brain'd guts, thou knotty-pated fool, thou whoreson, obscene, greasy tallow-catch—"
5. ". . . scurvy, old, filthy, scurvy lord!"
6. ". . . an ass-head and a cox-comb and a knave, a thin-fac'd knave, a gull!"
7. ". . . thou sodden-witted lord! Thou hast no more brain than I have in my elbows, an asinico may tutor thee."

a. Coriolanus to the mob

b. Thersites to Ajax

c. Parolles about Lafeu

d. Portia to Nerissa about a suitor

e. Prospero to Ariel

f. Touchstone to Corin

g. Clifford to the Duke of Gloucester

8. "Truly, thou art damn'd, like an ill-roasted egg, all on one side."

h. Lysander to Hermia

9. "God made him, and therefore let him pass for a man."

i. Sir Toby Belch to and about Sir Andrew Aguecheek

10. "Hence, heap of wrath, foul indigested lump, As crooked in the manners as thy shape!"

j. Doll Tearsheet to Pistol

11. "Away, you cutpurse rascal! You filthy bung . . ."

k. King Lear to Goneril

12. "Thou art a bile, A plague-sore, or embossed carbuncle, In my corrupted blood."

l. Hal to Falstaff

QUIZ #13
GENERATIONS

Match the parent listed at left to the offspring at right.

1. Baptista
2. Northumberland
3. Cymbeline
4. Brabantio
5. Leontes
6. Frederick
7. Regnier
8. An old shepherd
9. Constance
10. John of Gaunt
11. Salisbury

a. Margaret
b. Henry Beauford
c. Henry, Earl of Richmond
d. Guiderius
e. Antipholus
f. Martius
g. Anne
h. Thaisa
i. Hero
j. Warwick
k. Arthur

12.	Sir William Stanley	l.	Celia
13.	Calchas	m.	Hotspur
14.	Emilia	n.	Mamillius
15.	Volumnia	o.	Desdemona
16.	Margaret	p.	Proteus
17.	Simonides	q.	Joan of Pucelle
18.	Leonato	r.	Cressida
19.	Antonio	s.	Lucentio
20.	Vincentio	t.	Bianca

QUIZ #14
A MIDSUMMER NIGHT'S DREAM

This play may be Shakespeare's most popular comedy, a blending of multiple levels of life into one grand confection. Here are questions about several points of interest.

1. When Hermia refuses to marry Demetrius, what two alternatives does Theseus give her?
2. Identify the speaker: "The course of true love never did run smooth."
3. What are the names of the six "mechanicals"? And what are their professions?
4. What is Bottom's first name?
5. By what other name is Puck known?
6. What is the object of contention between Oberon and Titania?
7. Identify the speaker: "Who will not change a raven for a dove?"
8. Name the speaker and the addressee: "Thou art as wise as thou art beautiful."
9. What are the names of the four fairies who attend Bottom?
10. Identify the speaker: "Lord, what fools these mortals be!"

11. Identify the speaker:
    "I never heard
    So musical a discord, such sweet thunder."
12. According to Bottom, why shall his dream be called "Bottom's Dream"?
13. What two foods does Bottom warn his fellow actors about consuming?
14. According to Theseus, what three individuals are "of imagination all compact"?
15. Who, while watching the production of "Pyramus and Thisby," comments, "Beshrew my heart, but I pity the man"?

QUIZ #15
PLAYERS

For more than 400 years, Shakespeare's parts have been the pinnacle to which actors aspire. Here are descriptions of some of his most eminent interpreters. Name them.

1. This member of Shakespeare's company gave the first performances of such tragic roles as Hamlet, King Lear, and Othello.
2. This member of Shakespeare's company was a great comic player, physical and earthy, and probably the first to enact Bottom and Dogberry. He left the company in 1599, possibly because of a tendency to ad-lib.
3. This actor took over from the one described in question 2. He was smaller and more musical, and for him Shakespeare created Feste in *Twelfth Night* and the Fool in *King Lear*.
4. This actor dominated the London stage in the middle of the eighteenth century. As manager of the Drury Lane

Theater, he ended the practice of having spectators on stage and brought such innovations as realistic scenery.

5. Throughout the late eighteenth and early nineteenth centuries, this actress performed such roles as Desdemona, Ophelia, and Lady Macbeth, the last part for which she won greatest acclaim. She was also the first actress to play Hamlet. (Her name is attached to a fictional award in a famous movie about the theater. Name the movie.)

6. In the early nineteenth century, this flamboyant star specialized in villainous parts, particularly Shylock and Richard III. He collapsed during a performance of *Othello*, then died a few weeks later.

7. This nineteenth-century actor was noteworthy for restoring Shakespearean texts, which for centuries had been abridged and altered to fit the tastes of audiences and actors. In 1849, his rivalry with American actor Edwin Forrest resulted in the Astor Place riot, when anti-English protesters stormed a theater, a calamity that left twenty-two people dead.

8. This star was the leading American actor of his day, but his career was temporarily halted by his brother's act of political mayhem. He later retook the stage, making the role of Hamlet particularly compelling.

9. This man was the leading Shakespearean actor of the late nineteenth century and the first of his profession to be knighted. His Shylock, a dignified, even aristocratic, victim, was particularly influential.

10. The first successful black actor, this man was acclaimed as the outstanding American performer on the London stage during the nineteenth century. In addition to playing Othello and Aaron, he gave noted performances of Lear, Hamlet, and Shylock.

11. This woman was regarded as the leading Shakespearean actress of the late nineteenth and early twentieth centuries. Her greatest successes included Imogen, Portia, and Lady Macbeth. Her great-nephew was Sir John Gielgud.

12. This matinee idol played Hamlet in New York in 1925, offering the longest run, 101 performances, seen until that time.
13. In 1935, these two actors starred in the longest recorded run of *Romeo and Juliet*. One played Romeo, the other Mercutio. Six weeks later they switched parts.
14. This prodigious talent began his career in the 1930s, directing such controversial stage productions as a *Macbeth* set in Haiti with an all-black cast and a *Julius Caesar* set in fascist Italy. He later directed and acted in film versions of *Othello*, *Macbeth*, and his version of the Henriad.
15. In 2004, this British actor's King Lear was acclaimed by the members of the Royal Shakespeare Company as the greatest Shakespearean performance ever. On several occasions he rejected the offer of a knighthood, explaining that the title "Mr." was sufficient.

QUIZ #16
RICHARD II

The deposition of Richard II from the throne of England began eighty years of internal conflict, including the War of the Roses. Here are some questions about Shakespeare's version of the king's final years.

1. Whose murder is the subject of contention between Bullingbrook and Mowbray?
2. After Mowbray is sentenced to exile, what does he claim he will miss most?
3. What military enterprise does Richard intend to finance with money from Gaunt's treasury?
4. Bullingbrook is also known as the Duke of _____.

5. Identify the speaker of these words about Richard:
    ". . . I see thy glory like a shooting star
    Fall to the base earth from the firmament."

6. In what castle does Richard take refuge after his return from war?

7. Supply the next two lines spoken by Richard that follow these:
    ". . . And that small model of the barren earth
    Which serves as paste and cover to our bones."

8. What threat does Bullingbrook articulate if Richard does not repeal Bullingbrook's banishment and return his lands?

9. What flower does the Gardener plant in honor of the Queen's tears?

10. "O, if you raise this house against this house,
    It will the woefullest division prove
    That ever fell upon the cursed earth."
    Who utters this prophesy?

11. When Richard is about to surrender to Bullingbrook, to what does he compare the crown?

12. In what lines does Richard echo Marlowe's *Dr. Faustus*?

13. "I pardon him as God shall pardon me."
    Of whom is Henry IV speaking?

14. In what castle is Richard imprisoned?

15. "I am the King's friend, and will rid his foe."
    Who is speaking?

QUIZ #17
THE PLAYWRIGHT AND HIS WORLD

Here are some tidbits about Shakespeare's family and background, as well as his times and contemporaries.

1. April 23 is accepted as Shakespeare's birthday. In what year was he born?
2. What other noted dramatist was born that same year?
3. What world-famous sculptor and what bulwark of the Reformation also died that year?
4. What was the name of Shakespeare's father, and what was his profession? What was the maiden name of Shakespeare's mother?
5. When and whom did Shakespeare marry? Name their children.
6. When did Shakespeare publish his narrative poems *Venus and Adonis* and *The Rape of Lucrece*? To whom did he dedicate them?
7. What was the original name of the acting company with which Shakespeare is most associated? What was the company's later name?
8. Approximately how many spectators did the Globe Theatre hold? When did it burn down?
9. When did Shakespeare die? What piece of furniture did his will dictate be left to his wife?
10. What words did Shakespeare write to be inscribed on his gravestone?
11. In what year did the first Folio appear? Which of Shakespeare's plays was not included?
12. When did the Puritans succeed in shutting down London's playhouses?
13. In what year did Queen Elizabeth take the throne? In what year did she die?
14. Who succeeded her?
15. Who instigated "The Gunpowder Plot," and what was it?
16. What infamous Russian ruler died in 1584?
17. When did Tinoretto paint "The Last Supper"?
18. Who married John Rolfe in 1614?
19. What famous book of personal reflections appeared in France in 1580?
20. What scientist, born the same year as Shakespeare, appeared before the Inquisition in 1615?

QUIZ #18
WHO'S WHO (III)

Here's one more set of character descriptions, including some figures who are downright obscure. Identify the characters.

1. This man is hacked to death before he speaks a single word.
2. This young man escapes an attack authorized by a ruthless king.
3. This veteran knight tries to protect a girl but is no match for a band of outlaws.
4. This man urges the cold-blooded murder of three great leaders, but after his plan is rejected, he disappears, never to be heard from again.
5. This tavern worker rushes back and forth to comic effect, but his plight also reflects the subtle ruthlessness of his royal tormentor.
6. This courtier has the job of furnishing acts for entertainment.
7. This man uses pseudo-scientific nonsense to condemn an innocent man to the charge of madness. Eventually the accuser earns a well-deserved beating.
8. This simple man speaks courageously, albeit unknowingly, to a king. He challenges the king to a duel, but his more important role is to articulate sentiments about warfare and royal responsibility.
9. This warrior repeatedly tries to kill his greatest enemy, then joins forces with him, but inevitably their enormous egos clash.
10. This woman urges her brother-in-law to defend his family's honor, but he refuses.
11. This rascally henchman thwarts a marriage but is overcome by remorse and confesses.
12. This wife loves her husband so much that she wants to join him in battle.

13. This king sings when he dies.
14. This woman is murdered, then returns as a ghost to haunt her husband.
15. This pirate captures and eagerly kills an unscrupulous and lascivious nobleman.

QUIZ #19
KINGS AND SUCH (I)

Royalty is at the core of Shakespearean drama, for the welfare of a kingdom is often a direct consequence of the quality of leadership. Here are descriptions of ten authority figures. Match the lines to the appropriate sovereign. Try to name the speaker as well.

1. "'Tis his own blame hath put himself from rest,
   And must needs taste his folly."
2. "Therefore in fierce tempest is he coming,
   In thunder and in earthquake, like a Jove . . ."
3. "If he be so resolv'd,
   I can o'ersway him; for he loves to hear
   That unicorns may be betray'd with trees,
   And bears with glasses, elephants with holes . . ."
4. "We do not know
   How he may soften at the sight o' th' child:
   The silence often of pure innocence
   Persuades when speaking fails."
5. "I know not whether God will have it so
   For some displeasing service I have done,

a. Claudius

b. Richard III

c. Timon

d. Lear

e. Julius Caesar

That in his secret doom, out of my
blood
He'll breed revengement and a scourge
for me . . ."

6. "Now does he feel   f. Henry IV
His secret murthers sticking on his
hands;
Now minutely revolts upbraid his faith-
breach . . ."

7. "You taught me language, and my   g. Macbeth
profit on 't
Is, I know how to curse."

8. "The King doth wake to-night and   h. Leontes
takes his rouse,
Keeps wassail, and the swagg'ring
up-spring reels;"

9. "And is it thus? repays he my deep   i. Prospero
service
With such contempt? Made him I king
for this?"

10. "The middle of humanity thou never   j. Henry V
knewest, but the extremity of both
ends."

QUIZ #20
WHAT'S IN A NAME? (I)

So mused Juliet. Here are appellations common to at least two
of Shakespeare's plays, followed by the number of plays in which
they are found. Supply the titles.

1. Portia (2)
2. Brutus (2)

3. Sebastian (2)
4. Bianca (2)
5. Margaret (5)
6. Angelo (2)
7. Maria (2)
8. Paris (2)
9. Claudio (3)
   Note: one character by this name is sometimes referred to as "Claudius."
10. Mariana (2)
11. Helena (2)
12. Antonio (5)
13. Katherine or Katherina (4)
14. Petruchio (2)
15. Buckingham (3)
16. Pompey (2)
17. Duke of Burgundy (3)
18. Ferdinand (2)
19. Somerset (2)
20. Helen (2)

QUIZ #21
COLLEAGUES AND RIVALS

The late fifteenth and early sixteenth centuries are considered a golden age of drama. We tend to think primarily of Shakespeare, but he was only one, albeit the best, of a gifted group of playwrights. Here's a list of twelve famous works of the time. Match each to its author.

1. *Edward II*
2. *The Old Wives' Tale*
3. *The Spanish Tragedy*
4. *Bussy D'Ambois*

a. Thomas Dekker
b. John Ford
c. Beaumont and Fletcher
d. Thomas Middleton

5. *The White Devil*   e. George Peele
6. *The Revenger's Tragedy*   f. John Marston
7. *The Shoemaker's Holiday*   g. John Webster
8. *Friar Bacon and Friar   h. George Chapman
   Bungay*
9. *Women Beware Women*   i. Thomas Kyd
10. *Gammer Gurton's Needle*   j. Robert Greene
11. *'Tis Pity She's a Whore*   k. Ben Jonson
12. *The Malcontent*   l. Christopher Marlowe
13. *Sejanus*   m. Cyril Tourneur
14. *Ralph Roister Doister*   n. William Stephenson
15. *The Knight of the   o. Nicholas Udall
    Burning Pestle*

QUIZ #22
HAMLET

No work of art has been more analyzed than this one, and no character has been more discussed than the title figure. Try to answer these questions.

1. According to Marcellus, upon what sound did the Ghost quickly depart?
2. Whom does Claudius dispatch as emissaries to Norway?
3. Complete these aphoristic lines of Polonius:
   a. "Be thou familiar _____."
   b. "Give every man thine ear _____."
   c. "Take each man's censure _____."
   d. "This above all: _____

   _____

   _____."
4. What poison did Claudius pour in old Hamlet's ear?
5. "Let us go in together,
   And still your fingers on your lips, I pray."

What lines follow these?

6. On what events does Gertrude blame Hamlet's state of mind?

7. "I'll have grounds
   More relative than this . . ."
   What lines follow these?

8. What line precedes this one: ". . . why wouldst thou be a breeder of sinners?"

9. What stage role does Polonius claim he played?

10. In the performance of "The Murder of Gonzago," who is Lucianus?

11. Whom does Hamlet call a "delicate and tender prince"?

12. "Conscience and grace, to the profoundest pit!
    I dare damnation."
    Who says these words?

13. With what event does the gravedigger associate the birth of Hamlet thirty years earlier?

14. What object did Hamlet have with him to promote the execution of Rosencrantz and Guildenstern?

15. Whom does Hamlet call "this water-fly"?

QUIZ #23
WOMEN

Although male roles dominate Shakespeare's plays, some of his women characters are extraordinary presences. Here are quotations that reflect the range of Shakespeare's female figures. Match each quotation to the speaker.

1. "When I am dead, good wench,
   Let me be us'd with honor;
   strew me over

    a. Andromache

With maiden flowers, that all
the world may know
I was a chaste wife to my
grave."

2. "I have made strong proof of   b. Desdemona
my constancy,
Giving myself a voluntary
wound
Here, in the thigh: can I
bear that with patience,
And not my husband's
secrets?"

3. "Nay, when I have a suit   c. Cleopatra
Wherein I mean to touch
your love indeed,
It shall be full of poise and
difficult weight,
And fearful to be granted."

4. "Hang him instantly."   d. Juliet
5. "When you durst do it, then   e. Rosalind
you were a man . . ."

6. "What do you tremble? are   f. Katherine (*Henry VIII*)
you all afraid?
Alas, I blame you not, for
you are mortal,
And mortal eyes cannot
endure the devil."

7. "O, be persuaded! do not   g. Regan
count it holy
To be hurt by being just . . ."

8. "Love is merely a madness,   h. Lady Anne
and I tell you deserves as
well a dark house and a whip
as madmen do . . ."

9. "No more but e'en a   i. Portia
woman, and commanded
By such poor passion as the
maid that milks
And does the meanest
chares."

10. "Blister'd be thy tongue   j. Lady Macbeth
For such a wish! he was not
    born to shame:
Upon his brow shame is
    asham'd to sit . . ."

QUIZ #24
SCRAMBLE

What self-respecting quiz book would be complete without one scramble? Here are twenty names from Shakespeare's plays, but with letters confused. What are the names?

1. SPOERRPO
2. RECOCI
3. NASCASARD
4. WENELGDRO
5. RATSCOD
6. NOVILOBE
7. ORUTHI
8. NERFSHOLOE
9. DUPILES
10. LANDONAIB
11. NISTRAFBRO
12. MCRINAHA
13. EBNORO
14. CIVDOOLO
15. EDABSCILAI
16. CRITOULN
17. ROCRAMSIM
18. LUDAPPNH
19. HALATRID
20. USCOMINI

QUIZ #25
HENRY IV, PARTS 1 AND 2

These two plays, though often produced or read separately, are unified by theme and character. Here are some questions about a variety of textual details.

1. To what goddess does Falstaff claim fidelity?
2. Who suggests robbing Falstaff at Gadshill?
3. Who is Hotspur's brother-in-law?
4. Whom does Falstaff describe as that "sprightly Scot of Scots"?
5. What four words of Prince Hal foreshadow his inevitable break with Falstaff?
6. Identify the speaker: "I can call spirits from the vasty deep."
7. Who says the following words to Hotspur? "You stand against anointed majesty."
8. "If he outlive the envy of this day,
   England did never owe so sweet a hope,
   So much misconstrued in his wantonness."
   Who says these words about Prince Hal?
9. What does Falstaff pull from his case at Shrewsbury?
10. Which of the conspirators does Henry IV condemn to death?
11. Who tells Northumberland about Hotspur's fate?
12. "You that are old consider not the capacities of us that are young . . ."
    Who is speaking?
13. Who are Fang and Snare?
14. Who are the four sons of Henry IV?
15. What is Poins's first name?
16. Who is "the foul-mouth'd'st rogue in England"?
17. What is the name of the tailor who vows that in war "I will do my good will, sir, you can have no more"?

18. "... He drinks no wine." Of whom is Falstaff speaking?
19. "... Be it thy course to busy giddy minds
    With foreign quarrels, that action, hence borne out,
    May waste the memory of the former days."
    Who is counseling whom?
20. "I have long dreamt of such a kind of man,
    So surfeit-swell'd, so old, and so profane . . ."
    What lines precede these?

QUIZ #26
LOVERS (I)

No playwright has dramatized romance as movingly and memo-
rably as Shakespeare. Here is the first of two quizzes about lovers. This one offers ten declarations of passion. Match the lines
to the speaker, then name the object of affection.

1. "Mine ear is much enamored of thy note: a. Petruchio
   So is mine enthralled to thy shape . . ."
2. "Lord of lords!   b. Hamlet
   O infinite virtue, com'st thou smiling
      from
   The world's great snare uncaught?"
3. "If I profane with my unworthiest hand   c. Miranda
   This holy shrine. The gentle sin is this,
   My lips, two blushing pilgrims, ready
      stand
   To smooth that rough touch with a
      tender kiss."
4. "Your beauty, that did haunt me in my   d. Lorenzo
      sleep
   To undertake the death of all the world,
   So I might live one hour in your sweet
      bosom."

5. "Here we will sit, and let the sounds of music
   Creep in our ears."

6. "If it were now to die,
   T'were now to be most happy . . ."

7. "I will live in thy heart, die in thy lap,
   and be buried in thy eyes; and moreover
   I will go with thee to thy uncle's."

8. ". . . For thou art pleasant, gamesome,
   passing courteous
   But slow in speech, yet sweet as spring-
   time flowers."

9. "Forty thousand brothers
   Could not with all their quantity of love
   Make up my sum."

10. "I might call him
    A thing divine, for nothing natural
    I ever saw so noble."

e. Benedick

f. Romeo

g. Cleopatra

h. Othello

i. Richard III

j. Titania

QUIZ #27
VILLAINS

Shakespeare's plays offer a compelling gallery of miscreants, often characterized as "Machiavels," in honor of the Italian statesman who wrote *The Prince*, and whose name has become synonymous with crafty machination. Match each sentiment to the speaker.

1. "I cannot hide what I am: I must
   be sad when I have cause, and
   smile at no man's jests; eat when
   I have stomach, and wait for no
   man's leisure; sleep when I am

a. Aaron

drowsy, and tend on no man's
business; laugh when I am
merry, and claw no man in his
humor."

2. "To quicken your increase, I will   b. Edmund
   beget
   Mine issue of your blood upon
   your daughter."

3. "I will be bright, and shine in   c. Antonio
   pearl and gold,
   To wait upon this new-made
   empress."

4. "Virtue? A fig! 'tis in ourselves   d. Iachimo
   that we are thus or thus."

5. "The wheel is come full circle, I   e. Richard III
   am here."

6. "O wretched state! O bosom   f. Don John
   black as death!"

7. "Be reveng'd,   g. Duke of Gloucester
   Or she that bore you was no
   queen, and you
   Recoil from your great stock."

8. "My strong imagination sees a   h. Angelo
   crown
   Dropping upon thy head."

9. "Why, I can smile, and murther   i. Claudius
   whiles I smile,
   And cry 'Content' to that which
   grieves my heart,
   And wet my cheeks with artificial
   tears,
   And frame my face to all
   occasions."

10. "What's this? What's this? Is this   j. Iago
    her fault, or mine?
    The tempter, or the tempted,
    who sins most, ha?"

QUIZ #28
CLOWNS AND WITS

Among the most ingratiating characters in Shakespeare's plays are the clowns: both the bumblers, who offer unlikely insight, and the wits, who comment with telling perception. Match the sentiment with the speaker.

1. "O, 'tis a foul thing when a cur cannot keep himself in all companies!"

   a. Feste

2. "But if the water come to him and drown him, he drowns not himself; argal, he that is not guilty of his own death shortens not his own life."

   b. Bottom

3. "When thou clovest thy crown I th' middle and gav'st away both parts, thou bor'st thine ass on thy back o'er the dirt."

   c. Dogberry

4. ". . . it is a wise father that knows his own child."

   d. Fool (*King Lear*)

5. "Why, if thou never wast at court, thou never saw'st good manners; if thou never saw'st good manners, then thy manners must be wicked, and wickedness is sin, and sin is damnation."

   e. Clown (*Antony and Cleopatra*)

6. "Let her hang me! He that is well hang'd in
This world needs to fear no colors."

   f. Launce

7. "I wish you all joy of the worm."

   g. Launcelot Gobbo

8. "And yet, to say the truth, reason and love keep little company together now-a-days."

h. Porter (*Macbeth*)

9. "Therefore much drink may be said to be an equivocator with lechery . . ."

i. Gravedigger

10. "But, masters, remember that I am an ass; though it be not written down, yet forget not that I am an ass."

j. Touchstone

QUIZ #29
WORDS, WORDS, WORDS (I)

So speaks Hamlet. In drama, and in Shakespeare's plays in particular, nothing reveals characters so profoundly as their language. Here is the first of three similar quizzes. Below are ten groups of lines, with each set spoken by one character. Identify that character.

1. "The bow is bent and drawn, make from the shaft."   (I, i, 143)

   "I will say nothing."   (III, ii, 38)

   "Am I in France?"   (IV, vii, 75)

2. "But 'twas thy heavenly face that set me on."   (I, ii, 182)

   "I am not in the giving vein to-day."   (IV, ii, 116)

   "I shall despair; there is no creature loves me,
   And if I die no soul will pity me."   (V, iii, 200–201)

3. "It is so indeed, he is no less than a stuff'd man.

But for the stuffing—well, we are all (I, i, 58–60)
mortal."
"You kill me to deny it. Farewell." (IV, i, 291)
"And I pray thee now tell me, for (V, ii, 59–61)
which of my bad parts didst thou first
fall in love with me?"
4. "How high a pitch his resolution (I, i, 109)
soars!"
"Now put it, God, in the physician's
mind
To help him to his grave (I, iv, 59–61)
immediately!"
"I wasted time, and now doth time (V, v, 49)
waste me . . ."
5. "He after honor hunts, I after love:
He leaves his friends, to dignify them
more;
I leave myself, my friends, and all, for (I, i, 63–65)
love."
"O, but I love his lady too too much,
And that's the reason I love him so (II, iv, 205–206)
little."
"I'll force thee yield to my desire." (V, iv, 58)
6. "In following him, I follow but myself (I, i, 58)
. . ."
"Are you a man?" (III, iii, 374)
"Demand me nothing; what you
know, you know:
From this time forth I never will (V, ii, 303–304)
speak word."
7. "Lie there, my art. Wipe thou thine (I, ii, 25)
eyes, have comfort."
"All thy vexations (IV, i, 5–7)
Were but my trials of thy love, and
thou
Hast strangely stood the test."
"The rarer action is
In virtue than in vengeance." (V, i, 27–28)

8. "Ha, majesty! How high thy glory
      tow'rs
   When the rich blood of kings is set on   (II, i, 350–351)
      fire!"
   "Since kings break faith upon
      commodity,
   Gain, be my lord, for I will worship   (II, i, 597–598)
      thee."
   "This England never did, nor never
      shall,
   Lie at the proud foot of a conqueror,
   But when it first did help to wound   (V, vii, 112–114)
      itself."

9. "First go with me to church and call
      me wife,
   And then away to Venice to your   (III, ii, 303–304)
      friend . . ."
   "Your wife would give you little
      thanks for that
   If she were by to hear you make the   (IV, i, 288–289)
      offer."
   "You should in all sense be much
      bound to him,
   For as I hear he was much bound for   (V, i, 136–137)
      you."

10. "A plague upon it when thieves   (II, ii, 27–28)
       cannot be true to one another!"
    "Do thou amend thy face, and I'll   (III, iii, 24–25)
       amend my life."
    "Lord, Lord, how this world is given   (V, iv, 145–146)
       to lying!"

QUIZ #30
THE MERCHANT OF VENICE

This controversial play is classified as a comedy, but its dark aspects not only prevent laughter but also anticipate Shakespeare's later plays. Here are a few questions about the play.

1. To what does Bassanio compare Portia's "sunny locks"?
2. What Biblical episode does Shylock relate to justify his profession?
3. "Our house is hell, and thou, a merry devil,
   Didst rob it of some taste of tediousness."
   Who speaks these words?
4. What does Lorenzo intend to take along with Jessica?
5. Who is the first suitor to try to choose the correct casket?
6. Who is the second suitor?
7. Complete the question: "Now what news on the _____?"
8. What is Shylock's answer to his own question: "If a Christian wrong a Jew, what should his sufferance be by Christian example?"
9. What possession of Jessica's has been traded for a monkey?
10. Whose clothes does Portia borrow to disguise herself for court?
11. "I am a tainted wether of the flock,
    Meetest for death . . ."
    Who is the speaker?
12. After the judgment of the court, what two stipulations does Antonio impose on Shylock?
13. "The man that hath no music in himself,
    Nor is not moved with concord of sweet sounds,
    Is fit for treasons, stratagems, and spoils . . ."
    Who is the speaker?
14. Supply the next line: "How far that little candle throws his beams!"
15. Who marries Nerissa?

QUIZ #31
BATTLES

A good deal of military action is dramatized in Shakespeare's plays. Here are ten famous encounters. Match each one to the play in which it occurs.

1. Orleans
2. St. Albans
3. Philippi
4. Bosworth Field
5. Gaultree
6. Agincourt
7. Tewksbury
8. Actium
9. Angiers
10. Shrewsbury

a. *Henry VI, Part 2*
b. *King John*
c. *Antony and Cleopatra*
d. *Henry VI, Part 3*
e. *Julius Caesar*
f. *Henry IV, Part 1*
g. *Richard III*
h. *Henry IV, Part 2*
i. *Henry VI, Part 1*
j. *Henry V*

QUIZ #32
HONOR

No single word resounds more ironically through Shakespeare's plays than "honor." Sometimes it suggests sterling morality, but in many other contexts, it is a convenient excuse for questionable action. Here are ten quotations about honor. Match each one to the speaker.

1. "If I lose mine honor,
   I lose myself; better I were not
      yours
   Than yours so branchless."

a. Henry V

2. "Thou hast affected the fine strains
   of honor,
   To imitate the graces of the gods
   . . ."

   b. Northumberland

3. "Alas, sweet wife, my honor is at
   pawn,
   And but my going, nothing can
   redeem it."

   c. Brutus

4. "By heaven, methinks it were an
   easy leap,
   To pluck bright honor from the
   pale-fac'd moon . . ."

   d. Hamlet

5. "For let the gods so speed me as I
   love
   The name of honor more than I
   fear death."

   e. Falstaff

6. "An honorable murderer, if you
   will;
   For nought I did in hate, but all in
   honor."

   f. Hector

7. "Rightly to be great
   Is not to stir without great
   argument,
   But greatly to find quarrel in a
   straw
   When honor's at the stake."

   g. Hotspur

8. "But if it be a sin to covet honor,
   I am the most offending soul
   alive."

   h. Antony

9. "Mine honor keeps the weather of
   my fate.
   Life every man holds dear, but the
   dear man
   Holds honor far more precious-
   dear than life."

   i. Volumnia

10. "Can honor set to a leg? No. Or
    an arm? No. Or take away the grief

    j. Othello

of a wound? No. Honor hath no
skill in surgery then? No. What is
honor? A word."

QUIZ #33
CRITICISM

No artist has been the subject of more study and evaluation than
Shakespeare. Below are the titles of classic works of criticism.
Provide the author of each work.

1. *Essay on the Dramatic Character of Falstaff* (1777)
2. *The Characters of Shakespeare's Plays* (1817)
3. "On the Knocking at the Gate in *Macbeth*" (1823)
4. *Shakespearean Tragedy* (1904)
5. *Prefaces to Shakespeare* (1927–1947)
6. *The Wheel of Fire* (1930)
7. *Shakespeare's Imagery and What It Tells Us* (1935)
8. *What Happens in Hamlet* (1935)
9. *Shakespeare* (1939)
10. *Shakespeare's History Plays* (1944)
11. *Hamlet and Oedipus* (1949)
12. *The Meaning of Shakespeare* (1951)
13. *The Common Pursuit* (1952)
14. *Shakespeare Our Contemporary* (1964)
15. *Shakespeare the Playwright: A Companion to the Complete Tragedies, Histories, Comedies, and Romances* (1991)

QUIZ #34
WORDS, WORDS, WORDS (II)

QUIZ #34
WORDS, WORDS, WORDS (II)

Here are more sets of speeches, each uttered by one character. This test is perhaps more challenging than the last.

1. "I would my father look'd but with my eyes." (I, i, 56)
    "If then true lovers have been ever cross'd,
    It stands as an edict in destiny." (I, i, 150–151)
    "'Lower'? hark again." (III, ii, 305)
2. "Come, if it be nothing, I shall not need spectacles." (I, ii, 34–35)
    "My dear lord,
    You know the fiery quality of the Duke,
    How unremovable and fix'd he is
    In his own course." (II, iv, 91–94)
    "I see it feelingly." (IV, vi, 149)
3. "We must not stint
    Our necessary actions in the fear
    To cope malicious censurers . . ." (I, ii, 76–78)
    "What sudden anger's this? How have I reap'd it?
    He parted frowning from me, as if ruin
    Leap'd from his eyes." (III, ii, 204–206)
    "Had I but serv'd my God with half the zeal
    I serv'd my king, He would not in mine age
    Have left me naked to mine enemies." (III, ii, 455–457)
4. "O, let him marry her." (I, iv, 49)
    "O, it is excellent

52 BARD GAMES: THE SHAKESPEARE QUIZ BOOK

To have a giant's strength; but it is
   tyrannous
To use it like a giant."   (II, ii, 107–109)
"O you beast!
O faithless coward! O dishonest
   wretch!
Wilt thou be made a man out of my   (III, i, 135–137)
   vice?"
5. "Wars is no strife
To the dark house and the detested   (II, iii, 291–292)
   wife."
"Love is holy,
And my integrity ne'er knew the
   crafts
That you do charge men with."   (IV, ii, 32–34)
"If she, my liege, can make me know
   this clearly,
I'll love her dearly, ever, ever, dearly." (V, iii, 315–316)
6. "I do think there is mettle in death,   (I, ii, 142–144)
which commits some loving act
upon her, she hath such a celerity
in dying."
"That I beheld
Mine eyes did sicken at the sight and
   could not
Endure a further view."   (III, x, 15–17)
"I fight against thee? No, I will go
   seek
Some ditch wherein to die; the foul'st
   best fits
My latter part of life."   (IV, vi, 36–38)
7. "My lord, he hath importun'd me
   with love
In honorable fashion."   (I, iii, 110–111)
"No, my good lord, but as you did
   command
I did repel his letters, and denied
His access to me."   (II, i, 105–107)

"Come,
my coach! Good night, ladies, good
  night. Sweet
ladies, good night, good night."   (IV, v, 71–73)

8. "May I with right and conscience   (I, ii, 96)
  make this claim?"
"I will weep for thee;
For this revolt of thine, methinks, is
  like
Another fall of man."   (II, ii, 140–142)
"Every subject's
duty is the King's, but every subject's   (IV, i, 176–177)
  soul is his own."

9. "Thou shouldst be mad;
And I, to make thee mad, do mock   (I, iv, 89–90)
  thee thus."
"My lord, cheer up your spirits, our
  foes are nigh,
And this soft courage makes your
  followers faint.
You promis'd knighthood to our
  forward son,
Unsheathe your sword and dub him   (II, ii, 56–59)
  presently."
"We will not from the helm to sit and
  weep,
But keep our course (though the
  rough wind say no)
From shelves and rocks that threaten   (V, iv, 21–23)
  us with wrack."

10. "I would not by my will have
  troubled you,
But since you make your pleasure of
  your pains,
I will no further chide you."   (III, iii, 1–3)
"Or am I mad, or else this is a dream."   (IV, i, 61)
"How have the hours rack'd and
  tortur'd me,
Since I have lost thee!"   (V, i, 219–220)

QUIZ #35
A MATTER OF IDENTITY

Here's a quickie. Identify as many of the following as you can, then explain what all have in common.

1. Rosaline (*Romeo and Juliet*)
2. Leah (*The Merchant of Venice*)
3. Sycorax (*The Tempest*)
4. Susan (*Romeo and Juliet*)
5. Antonio (*The Taming of the Shrew*)
6. Gerard de Narbon (*All's Well That Ends Well*)
7. Richard the Lionhearted (*King John*)
8. Macdonwald (*Macbeth*)
9. Sir Rowland de Boys (*As You Like It*)
10. Lord Scales and Lord Hungerford (*Henry VI, Part 1*)

QUIZ #36
HENRY V

This play dramatizes one of the titanic figures of English history. Yet Shakespeare does not simply glorify Henry's conquests, for warfare itself is dramatized as barbaric and bloody, while the King is portrayed as a great leader whose political skills buttress his military gifts. Here are a few questions about the play.

1. When Henry agrees to take on the French in warfare, what other forces does he expect to battle?
2. What ancient law is invoked to thwart Henry's claim on the French throne?

3. What notorious, if apocryphal, gift does the French ambassador present?
4. Who dies after being abandoned by Henry V?
5. What three conspirators does Henry V accuse, then summarily execute?
6. "Let us to France, like horse-leeches, my boys,
   To suck, to suck, the very blood to suck!"
   Who is speaking?
7. Who is jilted by Mistress Quickly when she marries Pistol?
8. What theft causes Henry to condemn the perpetrator to death?
9. "The empty vessel makes the greatest sound."
   Who is speaking?
10. The Duke of York, who in Act IV, Scene iii, volunteers to lead the King's forces, appeared in an earlier play. By what name was he called there?
11. On what day is the battle of Agincourt fought?
12. How many soldiers does Henry claim the French lost at Agincourt?
13. How many soldiers does Henry claim the English lost in the same conflict?
14. Who is forced to eat leek? And by whom?
15. How does Pistol's wife die?

QUIZ #37
SHAKESPEARE AND FILM

Shakespeare's plays have proved to be fascinating sources for movie makers. These questions offer evidence of the variety of their efforts.

1. An early filmed version of which of Shakespeare's comedies boasts the notorious credit "additional dialogue by Sam Taylor"?

2. *A Midsummer Night's Dream* was filmed in 1935 in Hollywood. Who directed the film? What child star played Puck? What leading man, known best for his gangster roles, played Bottom with surprising success? What crooner, who later played a hard-boiled detective, played Lysander? What comedian played Flute? What subsequent star of *Gone With the Wind* played Hermia?

3. When *Romeo and Juliet* was first given a Hollywood treatment, the leading actors were, to put the matter politely, mature for their parts. Who directed the film? Who played the title characters? Who nearly stole the film playing Mercutio?

4. When *As You Like It* was filmed in 1936, Laurence Olivier played Orlando. Who was his leading lady?

5. What comedian made a rare film success playing a conceited Shakespearian actor in the original version of *To Be or Not To Be*?

6. Laurence Olivier's *Henry V*, filmed in 1944, was intended to inspire the British forces. What actor gave a brilliant performance as the less than sterling character of Pistol?

7. In 1947, Ronald Colman won an Academy Award for starring as an actor whose role of Othello carries offstage. Name the movie.

8. A 1948 version of *Hamlet* won the Oscar for Best Picture. Laurence Olivier directed, and also won an Oscar for Best Actor. What eminent British composer wrote the score?

9. When *Julius Caesar* was filmed in 1953, it featured an all-star cast. Who played Antony? Brutus? Cassius? Who played Caesar? Calphurnia? Portia? Casca? Who directed the film?

10. What 1955 British gangster film was inspired by the plot of one of Shakespeare's tragedies?

11. What three world-famous Shakespearean stars worked for their only time on film together in *Richard III* (1955)? What role did each play? Who directed the film?

12. What Shakespearean play is the basis for the 1956 science fiction classic *Forbidden Planet*?

13. What did Orson Welles call his 1966 film based on the character of Falstaff?
14. In 1969 Paul Scofield starred in a spare, black-and-white version of *King Lear*. Who directed the film?
15. Who directed a particularly gory version of *Macbeth* in 1971?
16. In the 1971 film *Theatre of Blood*, a crazed actor kills his critics by recreating deaths from Shakespeare's plays. Who plays the actor? Who plays his daughter?
17. Who directed *Tempest*, the 1982 adaptation of Shakespeare's last play?
18. What Shakespearean tragedy is the basis for *Ran*, a 1985 Japanese film? Who directed the film?
19. Who directed the recent version of *The Tempest* called *Prospero's Books*?
20. Who directed the movie version of *Rosencrantz and Guildenstern Are Dead*?
21. *The Dresser* (1983) is adapted from a stage play in which the characters of King Lear and the Fool are paralleled by the offstage relationship of the distinguished tragic actor, known only as Sir, and the dresser who cares for him. Who wrote the play? Who plays Sir, the actor? And who plays the dresser?
22. What film version of a play by Shakespeare features cameo performances by Charlton Heston, Jack Lemmon, Robin Williams, and Billy Crystal?
23. Who played the title role in the most recent film adaptation of *Titus Andronicus*?
24. Who starred in a film that includes both discussion and performance of *Richard III*?
25. What two young actors starred in a contemporary version of *Romeo and Juliet*?
26. This portrait of male street hustlers, directed by Gus Van Sant and starring River Phoenix, borrowed passages verbatim from *Henry IV, Part 1*. Name the film.

27. *10 Things I Hate About You* set one of Shakespeare's most popular comedies in a contemporary high school. Name the play.
28. *A Thousand Acres*, based on a novel by Jane Smiley, is a modern Midwestern version of what Shakespearean tragedy?
29. This version of a Shakespeare comedy, updated to the 1930s, featured popular songs of that era interpolated into the script. Name the film.
30. The screenplay credit for this 2006 movie claimed that the film was inspired by *Twelfth Night*. Name the film.

QUIZ #38
LOVERS (II)

Here are passionate excerpts between lovers who are not so celebrated. Once again, match the declaration on the left with the speaker on the right, then name the recipient of such affection.

1. "If thou would have such a one, take me! and take me, take a soldier, take a soldier, take a king."

   a. Berowne

2. ". . . With these forc'd thoughts I prithee darken not
   The mirth o' th' feast. Or I'll be thine, my fair,
   Or not my father's . . ."

   b. Helena

3. "My gracious silence, hail!
   Wouldst thou have laugh'd had I come coffin'd home,
   That weep'st to see me triumph?"

   c. Florizel

4. ". . . For where thou art, there is the world itself, With every several pleasure in the world; And where thou art not, desolation."

    d. Regan

5. "But though I lov'd you well, I woo'd you not And yet, good faith, I wish'd myself a man, Or that we women had men's privilege Of speaking first."

    e. Lysander

6. "To me she speaks, she moves me for her theme: What, was I married to her in my dream?"

    f. Cressida

7. "The will of man is by his reason sway'd; And reason says you are the worthier maid."

    g. Antipholus

8. "Mistress, look on me, Behold the window of my heart, mine eye, What humble suit attends thy answer there. Impose some service on me for thy love."

    h. Suffolk

9. "'Twere all one That I should love a bright particular star And think to wed it, he is so above me."

    i. Henry V

10. "Now, sweet lord, You know the goodness I intend upon you: Tell me but truly, but then speak the truth, Do you not love my sister?"

    j. Coriolanus

QUIZ #39
POTPOURRI: THE COMEDIES

The Comedy of Errors, The Two Gentlemen of Verona,
Love's Labor's Lost, The Merry Wives of Windsor,
Much Ado About Nothing, As You Like It,
Twelfth Night

1. Complete Sir Toby Belch's line: "Does thou think because thou art virtuous . . ."
2. This confused servant, who thinks himself alternately scolded and exhorted by his master, muses: "Time is a very bankrout and owes more than he is worth to season." Name the servant.
3. This knight, seemingly the embodiment of chivalry, fails to protect his lady love when they are beset by a bunch of hapless outlaws. Name the knight.
4. Who are Anne Page's three suitors?
5. What woman is solicited by all three suitors to facilitate their courtship of Anne Page?
6. "Some are born great . . ." Complete this line, and identify the speaker.
7. This independent gentleman refuses to play traditional games of courtship: "No, I was not born under a rhyming planet, nor can I woo in festival terms." Still, he falls in love in spite of himself. Name the gentleman.
8. According to Jaques, what are the seven ages of man?
9. When Malvolio is imprisoned, what persona does Feste adopt in pretending to help?
10. What piece of jewelry does Antipholus of Ephesus agree to purchase from Angelo?
11. Whom does Sir Toby Belch marry?
12. "Are not these woods
    More free from peril than the envious court?"
    Name the exiled speaker.

13. Who devises the pageant of the Nine Worthies, then plays three parts himself?
14. Who finds himself disguised as Herne the Hunter?
15. Who finds herself in a case of mistaken identity, then pleads, "Prove true imagination, O prove true . . ."?
16. What are the Phoenix and the Porpentine?
17. Who overhears a conversation about herself, then reflects:
    "Can this be true?
    Stand I condemn'd for pride and scorn so much?"
18. This shepherd steps aside when the woman he loves falls for another, but eventually the shepherd's good will is rewarded. Name the shepherd.
19. Who tells her steward "O, you are sick of self-love," an evaluation that could apply to the speaker herself, as well as almost everyone else in the play?
20. What is the name of Launce's dog?

QUIZ #40
MACBETH

The shortest of Shakespeare's tragedies, *Macbeth* is an unparalleled portrait of ambition, crime, and guilt. Here are a few questions of interest.

1. Why is Banquo uncertain about the gender of the witches?
2. "Nothing in his life
   Became him like the leaving it."
   Of whom is Macbeth speaking?
3. What title does Duncan bestow on Malcolm?
4. Complete this line from Lady Macbeth as she muses about her husband:
   "Yet I do fear thy nature,
   It is too full __ __ __ __ __ __ . . ."

5. What reason does Lady Macbeth offer for her failure to kill Duncan?
6. After the murder, what word can Macbeth not utter?
7. Who discovers that Duncan has been murdered?
8. Where is Macbeth crowned?
9. Whom does Macbeth claim to assign to join the two Murderers?
10. At the banquet, where does the Ghost of Banquo sit?
11. What does Lady Macbeth describe as "the season of all natures"?
12. What line of the second Witch is also the title of a novel by Ray Bradbury?
13. When Macbeth meets the witches for the second time, what does he seek to know from them?
14. What three apparitions do the witches show Macbeth?
15. Before his own death at the hands of Macduff, whom does Macbeth kill in combat?

QUIZ #41
SUPPORTING PLAYERS

Match the servant on the left to the appropriate boss. (Note: this quiz is difficult.)

1. Flavius	a.	Adriana
2. Abraham	b.	Cassius
3. Leonardo	c.	Hero
4. Adam	d.	Nurse (*Romeo and Juliet*)
5. Reynaldo	e.	Shallow
6. Luce	f.	Dr. Caius
7. Balthasar	g.	Cressida
8. Curio	h.	Bassanio
9. Lavache	i.	Posthumus
10. Davy	j.	Oliver
11. Peter	k.	Polonius

12. Lucetta	l. Armado
13. Rugby	m. Countess of Rossillion
14. Ursula	n. Proteus
15. Pindarus	o. Olivia
16. Moth	p. Montague
17. Alexander	q. Orsino
18. Launce	r. Julia
19. Fabian	s. Timon
20. Pisanio	t. Portia

QUIZ #42
SOLILOQUIES (II)

Here's another set of private ruminations, these less well known. Once again, the task is to match the speech at left to the speaker at right.

1. ". . . but till all graces be in   a. Brutus
   one woman, one woman shall not come
   in my grace."
2. "O world, thy slippery turns! Friends now   b. Autolycus
   fast sworn,
   Whose double bosoms seems to wear one
   heart . . ."
3. "O God! methinks it were a happy life   c. Cressida
   To be no better than a homely swain . . ."
4. "Matrons, turn incontinent!   d. Berowne
   Obedience, fail in children! Slaves and
   fools,
   Pluck the grave wrinkled Senate from the
   bench,
   And minister in their steads!"
5. "Women are angels, wooing: e. Diana
   Things won are done, joy's soul lies in the
   doing."

6. "Now I do love her too,
   Not out of absolute lust (though
      peradventure
   I stand accomptant for as great a sin) . . ."

7. "I understand the business, I hear it. To
   have an open ear, a quick eye, and a
   nimble hand, is necessary for a cutpurse
   . . ."

8. "He had sworn to marry me
   When his wife's dead; therefore I'll lie
      with him
   When I am buried."

9. "Crown him that,
   And then I grant we put a sting in him
   That at his will he may do danger with."

10. "O, and I, forsooth, in love! I, that have
      been love's whip,
   A very beadle to a humorous sigh,
   A critic, nay, a night-watch constable,
   A domineering pedant o'er the boy,
   Than whom no mortal so magnificent!"

f. Henry VI

g. Iago

h. Coriolanus

i. Benedick

j. Timon

QUIZ #43
SOURCES

As Shakespeare was apparently content to rework other people's
stories, only rarely did he create original plots. Match the source
at left with the appropriate work.

1. A novella from Cinthio's
   Hecatommithi

2. Plutarch's *Life of
   Alcibiades*

a. *All's Well That Ends Well*

b. *The Merchant of Venice*

3. The story of Giletta
   of Narbona from
   Boccaccio's *Decameron*
4. Ovid's *Metamorphoses*
5. Robert Greene's novel
   Pandosto
6. Ser Giovanni's *Il Pecorone*
   (*The Simpleton*)
7. *Diana Enamorada* by
   Jorge de Montemayor
8. *Historia Danica* by Saxo
   Grammaticus
9. *The Menaechmi* by Plautus
10. *Confession Amantis* by
    John Gower
11. Honlinshed's *Chronicles*
12. A poem by Arthur Brooke

c. *Hamlet*

d. *The Comedy of Errors*
e. *Pericles*

f. *The Two Gentlemen
   of Verona*
g. *Othello*

h. *Romeo and Juliet*

i. *Timon of Athens*
j. *The Winter's Tale*

k. *A Midsummer
   Night's Dream*
l. *Macbeth*

QUIZ #44
POTPOURRI:
THE FIRST TETRALOGY

Henry VI, Parts 1, 2, 3, and *Richard III*

These four works, written early in Shakespeare's career, are an
unpolished but theatrical portrait of the War of the Roses. Here
are a few questions about the plays.

1. What title is borne by William de la Pole?
2. "I must not yield to any rites of love,
   For my profession's sacred from above."
   Who says these lines?

3. In *Henry VI*, whom does Warwick wish Edward to marry?
4. "The first thing we do, let's kill all the lawyers."
   Name the play and the speaker.
5. What one character appears in all four plays?
6. What is Stanley's actual title?
7. How many ghosts visit Richard III before his final battle?
   Name the ghosts.
8. Who is dismissed by whom as "a child, a silly dwarf"?
9. Who kills Prince Edward?
10. What imposter claims to have once been blind and now to be paralyzed?
11. Who is described by York as "a headstrong Kentishman"?
12. "Done like a Frenchman—turn and turn again!"
    Name the speaker and the object of scorn.
13. "Oft have I seen a hot o'erweening cur
    Run back and bit because he was withheld,
    Who, being suffered, with the bear's fell paw,
    Hath clapp's tail between his legs and cried . . ." (*Henry VI, Part 2*, V, i, 151–154)
    Why are these words particularly notable?
14. "Zounds, he dies!"
    Who says these words about whom?
15. What astronomical phenomenon appears before the surviving sons of York after the death of their father?
16. Who orders what cohort to "Call them again"?
17. "Die, damned wretch, the curse of her that bare thee;
    And as I thrust thy body in with my sword,
    So wish I, I might thrust thy soul to hell."
    Who is speaking of whom?
18. "Civil dissension is a viperous worm
    That gnaws the bowels of the commonwealth."
    Who offers this astute observation?
19. What infamous woman does Richard III pretend to blame for his withered arm?
20. In *Henry VI, Part 2*, Warwick claims, "What plain proceeding is more plain than this?" (II, ii, 53). To what genealogical controversy does he refer?

BROTHERS AND SISTERS

Here's another difficult one. Match the character at left with his or her sibling at right.

1.	Lady Percy	a.	Humphrey of Gloucester
2.	Luciana	b.	Lord Rivers
3.	Earl of Rutland	c.	Isabella
4.	Sebastian	d.	Deiphobus
5.	Paris	e.	Northumberland
6.	Oliver	f.	Quintus
7.	Alonso	g.	Don John
8.	Claudio	h.	Demetrius
9.	Duke of Exeter	i.	Orlando
10.	Lady Grey	j.	Guiderius
11.	Leonato	k.	Antonio
12.	Alarbus	l.	Sebastian
13.	Worcester	m.	Bishop of Winchester
14.	John of Lancaster	n.	Donalbain
15.	Lucius	o.	Mortimer
16.	Marquess of Dorset	p.	Ophelia
17.	Laertes	q.	Adriana
18.	Malcolm	r.	Duke of Clarence
19.	Imogen	s.	Viola
20.	Don Pedro	t.	Lord Grey

KINGS AND SUCH (II)

Here are descriptions of more royals, some a bit obscure. Again, match the quotation to the figure. For an additional challenge, name the speaker.

1. "May he live   a. Edward IV
Longer than I have time to tell his
years;
Ever belov'd and loving may his rule
be . . ."
2. "Would he were wasted, marrow,   b. Antiochus
bones, and all,
That from his loins no hopeful
branch may spring,
To cross me from the golden time I
look for!"
3. "Ere he would have hang'd a man   c. Richard II
for getting a hundred bastards, he
would have paid for the nursing a
thousand."
4. "Yet looks he like a king! Behold, his d. Margaret
eye,
As bright as is the eagle's, lightens
forth
Controlling majesty. Alack, alack, for
woe,
That any harm should stain so far a
show."
5. "Quarrel no more, but be prepar'd   e. Henry IV
to know
The purposes I bear; which are, or
cease,
As you shall give th' advice."
6. "Her peerless feature, joined with   f. Henry VI
her birth
Approves her fit for none but for a
king."
7. "Great King,   g. Henry VIII
Few love to hear the sins they love
to act;
'Twould braid yourself too near for
me to tell it."
8. "O, pardon me, my liege! but for my   h. Cleopatra
tears,

The moist impediments unto my
    speech,
I had forestall'd this dear and deep
    rebuke . . ."

9. "Ah, wretched man, would I have
    died a maid
    And never seen thee, never borne
    thee son . . ."

    i. John

10. "It was my breath that blew this
    tempest up
    Upon your stubborn usage of the
    Pope . . .
    Go I to make the French lay down
    their arms."

    j. Duke Vincentio

QUIZ #47
THE ROMAN TRAGEDIES

Titus Andronicus, Julius Caesar,
Antony and Cleopatra, Coriolanus

In these works, Shakespeare explores many of the themes that
dominate his plays about English history. Here are some challenging questions.

1. Name the eight conspirators against Julius Caesar.
2. Complete this quote of Caesar's: "I am as constant as
   __ __ __."
3. Whose body is identified by a ring that shines through
   darkness?
4. When Valeria talks of Martius's son, what animal does she
   describe him as consuming?
5. Who says, "The time of universal peace is near"?
6. From what precipice does the Roman mob threaten to toss
   Coriolanus?

7. How does Portia die?
8. Who says, "Away, slight man!"
9. Why, in Casca's words, are Murellus and Flavius put to death?
10. "Her love to both
    Would each to other and all loves to both
    Draw after her."
    Who is speaking? Whose love is in question?
11. "It is a part
    That I shall blush in acting, and might well
    Be taken from the people."
    Who is speaking? And of what "part"?
12. What lines precede these?
    "Of all the wonders that I yet have heard,
    It seems to me most strange that men should fear,
    Seeing that death, a necessary end,
    Will come when it will come."
13. How many sons of Titus Andronicus survive the play?
14. Who holds the sword as Brutus runs on it?
15. "He will to his Egyptian dish again."
    Who makes this prediction?
16. Who relates the tale of the belly?
17. Who strikes murderously at a fly?
18. How many times does Aufidius claim he has been defeated by Martius?
19. "None about Caesar trust but _____." Fill in the name that completes Antony's warning to Cleopatra.
20. "I do not cross you, but I will do so." Who is speaking to whom?

QUIZ #48
WORDS, WORDS, WORDS (III)

Here are more sets of quotations, each group selected from one play. Name that play. For those who seek a sterner test, name each speaker.

1. "She lov'd me for the dangers I had pass'd,
   And I lov'd her that she did pity them." — (I, iii, 167–168)
   "Hah! I like not that." — (III, iii, 35)
   "'Tis not a year or two shows us a man:
   They are all but stomachs, and we all but food;
   They eat us hungerly, and when they are full
   They belch us." — (III, iv, 103–106)
   "Commend me to my kind lord." — (V, ii, 125)
2. "The heavens themselves, the planets, and this centre
   Observe degree, priority, and place
   . . ." — (I, iii, 85–86)
   "Nay, if we talk of reason,
   Let's shut our gates and sleep.
   Manhood and honor
   Should have hare hearts, would they but fat their thoughts
   With this cramm'd reason . . ." — (II, ii, 46–50)
   "I do hate a proud man, as I do hate the engend'ring of toads." — (II, iii, 158–159)
   "If the son of a whore fight for a whore, he
   tempts judgment." — (V, vii, 21–22)
3. "I am not only witty in myself, but — (I, ii, 9–10)
   the cause that wit is in other men."

"Uneasy lies the head that wears a   (III, i, 31)
    crown."
"I promis'd you redress of these same
    grievances
Whereof you did complain, which,
    by mine honor,
I will perform with a most Christian   (IV, ii, 113–115)
    care."
"I never thought to hear you speak   (IV, v, 91)
    again."
4. "Sweet are the uses of adversity . . ."   (II, i, 12)
". . . we ripe and ripe,
And then from hour to hour, we ripe
    and ripe,
And thereby hangs a tale."   (II, vii, 26–28)
"There was no thought of pleasing   (III, ii, 266–267)
you when she was christen'd."
"Come, woo me, woo me; for now   (IV, i, 68–69)
I am in a holiday humor, and like
enough to consent."
5. "Some villain hath done me wrong."   (I, ii, 165)
"This seems a fair deserving, and
    must draw me
That which my father loses: no less
    than all.
The younger rises when the old doth   (III, iii, 23–25)
    fall."
"Oppressed nature sleeps."   (III, vi, 97)
"No cause, no cause."   (IV, vii, 74)
6. "Ay, my mother,
With all my heart I thank thee for my   (I, i, 269–270)
    father."
"What earthy name to interrogatories
Can taste the free breath of a sacred   (III, i, 147–148)
    king?"
"Life is as tedious as a twice-told tale
Vexing the dull ear of a drowsy man   (III, iv, 108–109)
    . . ."
"How green you are and fresh in this   (III, iv, 145)
    old world!"

7. "Either there is a civil strife in
heaven,
Or else the world, too saucy with the
gods,
Incenses them to send destruction."   (I, iii, 11–13)
"He wish'd today our enterprise
might thrive.
I fear our purpose is discovered."   (III, i, 16–17)
"Methinks there is much reason in   (III, ii, 108)
his sayings."
"He shall not live; look, with a spot I   (IV, i, 6)
damn him."
8. "If she be furnish'd with a mind so
rare,
She is alone th' Arabian bird, and I
Have lost the wager."   (I, vi, 16–18)
"His meanest garment?"   (II, iii, 150)
"I see a man's life is a tedious one,
I have tir'd myself; and for two
nights together
Have made the ground my bed. I
should be sick,
But that my resolution helps me."   (III, vi, 1–4)
"My daughter? what of her? Renew
thy strength;
I had rather thou shouldst live while
nature will
Than die ere I hear more. Strive,   (V, v, 150–152)
man, and speak."
9. "This castle hath a pleasant seat, the
air
Nimbly and sweetly recommends
itself
Unto our gentle senses."   (I, vi, 1–3)
"What, in our house?"   (II, iii, 88)
"Such welcome and unwelcome
things at once
'Tis hard to reconcile."   (IV, iii, 138–139)
"I have almost forgot the taste of   (V, v, 19)
fears."

10. "Too hot, too hot!"   (I, ii, 108)
   "This child was prisoner to the
      womb, and is
   By law and process of great Nature
      thence
   Freed and enfranchis'd . . ."   (II, ii, 57–59)
   "Yet Nature is made better by no
      mean
   But Nature makes that mean; so over
      that art
   Which you say adds to Nature, is an
      art
   That Nature makes."   (IV, iv, 89–92)
   "You gods, look down
   And from your sacred vials pour your
      graces
   Upon my daughter's head!"   (V, iii, 121–123)

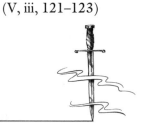

QUIZ #49
WHAT'S IN A NAME? (II)

Here's the second and more difficult installment of this quiz.
Once more you have a list of names common to more than one
play and the number of plays in which each name may be found.
Supply the titles.

1. Ross (2)
2. Stephano (2)
3. Cornelius (2)
4. Demetrius (3)
5. Ventidius (2)
6. Diomedes (2)
7. Vincentio (2)
8. Flavius (2)
9. Balthazar, or Balthasar (4)

10. Valentine (3)
11. Francisco (2)
12. Emilia, or Aemilia (3)
13. Lucilius (2)
14. Adrian (2)
15. Lucius (4)

QUIZ #50
SONGS

Shakespeare's plays contain a number of eloquent pieces. Match the lyrics to the singer.

1. "'Cuckoo, cuckoo'—O word of fear,
   Unpleasing to a married ear."

   a. Musicians near the Duke's palace

2. "Tell me where is fancy bred,
   Or in the heart or in the head?"

   b. Mercutio

3. "Full fadom five thy father lies,
   Of his bones are coral made . . ."

   c. Balthazar

4. "Blow, blow, thou winter wind,
   Thou art not so unkind
   As man's ingratitude . . ."

   d. Silence

5. "Who is Silvia? what is she,
   That all our swains commend her?"

   e. Armado

6. "Sigh no more, ladies, sigh no more,
   Men were deceivers ever . . ."

   f. Portia and musicians

7. "How should I your true love know
   From another one?
   By his cockle hat and staff,
   And his sandal shoon."

   g. Guiderius

8. "An old hare hoar,

   h. Ariel

And an old hare hoar,
Is very good meat in Lent;
But a hare that is hoar
Is too much for a score,
When it hoars ere it be spent."

9. "Do nothing but eat, and make   i. Ophelia
   good cheer,
   And praise God for the merry
   year,
   When flesh is cheap and females
   dear . . ."

10. "Fear no more the heat o' th'   j. Amiens
    sun,
    Nor the furious winter's rages,
    Thou thy worldly task hast done,
    Home art gone, and ta'en thy
    wages."

QUIZ #51
DEATH SCENES

Characters in Shakespeare's plays die in all sorts of ways, some
of them downright gruesome. To the left are ten circumstances
under which characters "shuffle off this mortal coil"; to the right
are the names of the characters. Match the circumstance to the
character.

1. is killed in one-on-one combat.   a. Duke of Clarence
2. is beheaded.   b. Chiron
3. is poisoned.   c. Rosencrantz
4. dies of grief.   d. Ragozine
5. is drowned in malmsey.   e. Cinna
6. jumps from castle battlement.   f. Joan of Pucelle
7. is executed in England.   g. Mamillius
8. is killed by a mob.   h. Arthur

9. is beheaded and baked.   i. Regan
10. is burned at the stake.   j. Hector

QUIZ #52
CLOSING LINES

Shakespeare's plays don't simply fade away. Even last lines matter, as these selections show. Match the final words to the appropriate play.

1. "Now civil wounds are stopp'd,   a. *Hamlet*
     peace lives again;
   That she may long live here,
     God say amen!"
2. "Think not on him till   b. *Richard II*
     to-morrow. I'll
   devise thee brave punishments
     for him.
   Strike up, pipers."
3. "The oldest hath borne most;   c. *As You Like It*
     we that are young
   Shall never see so much, nor live
     so long."
4. "Till then I'll sweat and seek   d. *Twelfth Night*
     about for eases,
   And at that time bequeath you
     my diseases."
5. "I'll make a voyage to the Holy   e. *Richard III*
     Land,
   To wash this blood off from my
     guilty hand.
   March sadly after, grace my
     mournings here,
   In weeping after this untimely
     bier."

6. "A great while ago the world
    began,
  With hey ho, the wind and the
    rain,
  But that's all one, our play is
    done,
  And we'll strive to please you
    every day."

f. *King John*

7. ". . . I am sure, as many as
  have good beards, or good
    faces, or sweet
  breaths, will for my kind offer,
    when I make
  curtsy, bid me farewell."

g. *The Tempest*

8. "Now these her princes are
    come home again,
  Come the three corners of the
    world in arms,
  And we shall shock them,
    Nought shall make us rue,
  If England to itself do rest but
    true."

h. *Troilus and Cressida*

9. "Go bid the soldiers shoot."

i. *King Lear*

10. "As you from crimes would
    pardon'd be,
  Let your indulgence set me free."

j. *Much Ado About
    Nothing*

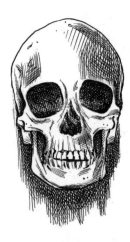

ANSWERS

ANSWERS

Introduction

Fifty-two quizzes, a fitting number about a man who probably died on April 23, 1616, his 52nd birthday.

1. Opening Lines

1. d. Barnardo establishes the theme of identity.
2. a. Henry IV clarifies the unrest in his kingdom.
3. h. Antonio communicates his chronic melancholy.
4. e. The Duke of Bedford mourns his dead brother, Henry V, and foreshadows the dissension that will torment his country.
5. c. Philo expresses disgust over Antony's neglect of duty and dalliance with Cleopatra.
6. g. The Chorus seeks a stage and voice grand enough to reveal the greatness of Henry V.
7. k. Under the guise of beneficence and patriotism, Saturninus seeks the support of the people.
8. l. Orsino luxuriates in his own decadence.
9. o. A gentleman reflects on the unhappy state of the kingdom.
10. n. Ferdinand, King of Navarre, reveals the egoism that drives all men.
11. b. Egeon awaits sentence for selling goods in enemy territory.
12. m. The speaker tries to establish an appropriately solemn tone.
13. i. Flavius berates the mob.
14. f. During the storm, the shipmaster calls for help.

15. j. The Countess of Rossillion blends happiness with despair.

2. Settings

1. d.	6. n.	11. h.
2. f.	7. o.	12. e.
3. l.	8. m.	13. i.
4. k.	9. g.	14. b.
5. j.	10. a.	15. c.

3. Name That Play (I)

1. *Henry V*
2. *Othello*
3. *All's Well That Ends Well*
4. *King John*
5. *Richard III*
6. *The Merry Wives of Windsor*
7. *The Tempest*
8. *Love's Labor's Lost*
9. *Henry VI, Part 2*
10. *Titus Andronicus*
11. *As You Like It*
12. *King Lear*
13. *The Taming of the Shrew*
14. *A Midsummer Night's Dream*
15. *Henry IV, Part 2*
16. *Julius Caesar*
17. *The Winter's Tale*
18. *Richard II*
19. *Henry VIII*
20. *Measure for Measure*

4. Who's Who (I)

1. Ajax (*Troilus and Cressida*)
2. Mowbray (*Richard II*)

3. Roderigo (*Othello*)
4. Talbot (*Henry VI, Part 1*)
5. Polonius (*Hamlet*)
6. Casca (*Julius Caesar*)
7. Olivia (*Twelfth Night*)
8. Lady Macduff (*Macbeth*)
9. Angelo (*Measure for Measure*)
10. Proteus (*The Two Gentlemen of Verona*)
11. Kent (*King Lear*)
12. Henry VI (*Henry VI, Part 3*)
13. Miranda (*The Tempest*)
14. Borachio (*Much Ado About Nothing*)
15. Iras (*Antony and Cleopatra*)

5. *Romeo and Juliet*

1. ". . . two hours' traffic of our stage" (Prologue, 12)
2. "Your lives shall pay the forfeit of the peace" (I, i, 97).
3. "She hath not yet seen the change of fourteen years" (I, ii, 9).
4. A servant asks him to read a list of guests (I, ii, 69).
5. Paris (I, iii, 76)
6. "The fairies' midwife" (I, iv, 54)
7. By his voice (I, v, 54)
8. "Deny thy father and refuse thy name . . ." (II, ii, 34).
9. "King of Cats" (III, i, 77)
10. Romeo (III, i, 136); after he has slain Tybalt
11. A ring (III, iii, 163)
12. Tybalt's ghost seeking out Romeo (IV, iii, 55)
13. Friar John
14. "Among a sisterhood of holy nuns" (V, iii, 157)
15. Her "statue in pure gold" (V, iii, 299)

6. Adaptations, Musical and Otherwise

1. *The Boys from Syracuse* (1938)
2. "Brush Up Your Shakespeare"; two gangsters
3. Stephen Sondheim, Jerome Robbins

---

4. *Twelfth Night*
5. Giuseppe Verdi, *Otello* (1887) and *Falstaff* (1893)
6. Felix Mendelssohn, *A Midsummer Night's Dream*
7. *Oberon*
8. *Sir John in Love*
9. *Romeo and Juliet*
10. Richard Wagner, *Measure for Measure*
11. Sir Edward Elgar
12. Beethoven (1807)
13. Edward Bond, *Lear*
14. Eugene Ionesco, *Macbett*
15. Flipping a coin; the coin repeatedly comes up "heads."
16. John Updike, *Gertrude and Claudius*
17. Paula Vogel
18. Fortinbras
19. *Antony and Cleopatra*
20. Arnold Wesker

7. Soliloquies (I)

1. c. (*Julius Caesar*, III, i, 256–257.
   Antony mourns over the body of the slain Caesar.)
2. f. (*Henry IV, Part 1*, I, ii, 216–217.
   Hal plots his future with characteristic political acumen.)
3. i. (*The Taming of the Shrew*, IV, i, 188–189.
   Petruchio explains his strategy for subduing Katherine.)
4. b. (*Hamlet*, II, ii, 571–573.
   Hamlet berates himself for his inaction.)
5. g. (*Romeo and Juliet*, III, ii, 10–13.
   As Juliet anticipates Romeo's arrival, her passion overflows.)
6. e. (*King Lear*, I, ii, 1–2.
   Edmund broods on his status as a bastard.)
7. h. (*Henry V*, IV, i, 233–236.
   Henry V ponders the burdens of kingship.)
8. a. (*Twelfth Night*, II, ii, 27–30.
   As Viola must refrain from pursuing her love for Orsino, her desperation is clear.)

9. j. (*Macbeth*, I, vii, 12.

Macbeth weighs the consequences of murdering Duncan.)

10. d. (*Richard II*, V, v, 42–43.

King Richard reflects on his failed reign.)

8. Disguises

1. Viola (*Twelfth Night*)
2. Vincentio (*Measure for Measure*)
3. Julia (*The Two Gentlemen of Verona*)
4. Celia (*As You Like It*)
5. Kent (*King Lear*)
6. Joan of Pucelle (*Henry VI, Part 1*)
7. Helena (*All's Well That Ends Well*)
8. Ferdinand, Berowne, Longaville, Dumaine (*Love's Labor's Lost*)
9. Tamora (*Titus Andronicus*)
10. Imogen (*Cymbeline*)
11. Portia (*The Merchant of Venice*)
12. Lucentio (*The Taming of the Shrew*)
13. Ford (*The Merry Wives of Windsor*)
14. Hero (*Much Ado About Nothing*)
15. Henry V (*Henry V*)

9. The Stage Itself

1. d. (*The Tempest*, IV, i, 148–150.

Prospero comments on the illusory and transitory aspects of theater.)

2. f. (*Macbeth*, V, v, 23–26.

After much violence and the death of his wife, Macbeth sees life as meaningless.)

3. e. (*King Lear*, IV, vi, 182–183.

Lear envisions the emptiness of existence.)

4. i. (*The Merchant of Venice*, I, i, 77–79.

Antonio seems to find pleasure in his own despondency.)

5. g. (*Antony and Cleopatra*, v, iii, 214–217.

Cleopatra anticipates how her passion for Antony will be mocked by future generations.)

6. c. (*Richard II*, V, ii, 23–25.

York describes Richard II's pitiable departure from the throne.)

7. h. (*Troilus and Cressida*, I, iii, 153–155.

Ulysses characterizes what he views as the disgraceful indolence of Achilles.)

8. b. (*A Midsummer Night's Dream*, V, i, 355–356.

Theseus graciously turns down Bottom's offer to present a proper conclusion to "Pyramis and Thisbe.")

9. j. (*Hamlet*, III, ii, 17–19.

Hamlet gives advice to the company of players, counsel that the Prince himself fails to follow during the subsequent performance. We should probably assume that the words also apply to members of Shakespeare's company who mangled his scripts.)

10. a. (*Julius Caesar*, III, i, 111–113.

Cassius revels in the death of Caesar, mistaken about how the assassination will be regarded by Rome. Yet he is ironically accurate about how the scene shall be reenacted throughout history.)

10. *The Taming of the Shrew*

1. Tinker
2. Bartholomew (Induction, i, 105)
3. ". . . to wive it wealthily" (I, ii, 75)
4. Minola (I, ii, 97)
5. The courting of Katherina (I, ii, 265)
6. Litio, "cunning in music and the mathematics" (II, i, 56)
7. The name taken by the disguised Lucentio (II, i)
8. Because he claims that "she mistook her frets" (II, i, 149)
9. Gremio
10. Biondello (III, ii, 43–63)
11. When he discards the newly made dress (IV, iii, 172)

12. Curtis (IV, i, 85)
13. Petruchio (IV, i, 208)
14. Vincentio (IV, v, 37)
15. "Such duty as the subject owes a prince . . ." (V, ii, 155–156)

11. Who's Who (II)

1. Poins (*Henry IV, Part 2*)
2. Saturninus (*Titus Andronicus*)
3. Audrey (*As You Like It*)
4. Gratiano (*The Merchant of Venice*)
5. Thersites (*Troilus and Cressida*)
6. The Duke of France (*King Lear*)
7. George, Duke of Clarence (*Richard III*)
8. Belarius (*Cymbeline*)
9. Parolles (*All's Well That Ends Well*)
10. Antonio (*The Tempest*)
11. Agrippa (*Antony and Cleopatra*)
12. Alexander Iden (*Henry VI, Part 2*)
13. Captain MacMorris (*Henry V*)
14. Feeble (*Henry IV, Part 2*)
15. Lewis the Dauphin (*Henry V*)

12. Insults

1. e. (*The Tempest*, I, ii, 258)
2. h. (*A Midsummer Night's Dream*, III, ii, 328–330)
3. a. (*Coriolanus*, III, iii, 120–122)
4. l. (*Henry IV, Part 1*, II, iv, 226–228)
5. c. (*All's Well That Ends Well*, II, iii, 236)
6. i. (*Twelfth Night*, V, i, 206–207)
7. b. (*Troilus and Cressida*, II, i, 43–45)
8. f. (*As You Like It*, III, ii, 37–38)
9. d. (*The Merchant of Venice*, I, ii, 56–57)
10. g. (*Henry VI, Part 2*, V, i, 157–158)
11. j. (*Henry IV, Part 2*, II, iv, 127)
12. k. (*King Lear*, II, iv, 223–225)

13. Generations

1. t. (*The Taming of the Shrew*)
2. m. (*Henry IV, Parts 1 and 2*)
3. d. (*Cymbeline*)
4. o. (*Othello*)
5. n. (*The Winter's Tale*)
6. l. (*As You Like It*)
7. a. (*Henry VI, Part 1*)
8. q. (*Henry VI, Part 1*)
9. k. (*King John*)
10. b. (*Henry IV, Part 1, Henry VI, Part 1*)
11. j. (*Henry VI, Parts 1, 2, and 3*)
12. c. (*Richard III*)
13. r. (*Troilus and Cressida*)
14. e. (*The Comedy of Errors*)
15. f. (*Coriolanus*)
16. g. (*The Merry Wives of Windsor*)
17. h. (*Pericles*)
18. i. (*Much Ado About Nothing*)
19. p. (*Two Gentlemen of Verona*)
20. s. (*The Taming of the Shrew*)

14. *A Midsummer Night's Dream*

1. "Either to die the death, or to abjure
   For ever the society of men." (I, i, 65–66)
2. Lysander (I, i, 134)
3. Quince is a carpenter.
   Bottom is a weaver.
   Flute is a bellows mender.
   Snout is a tinker.
   Snug is a joiner.
   Starveling is a tailor.
4. Nick (I, ii, 16)
5. Robin Goodfellow (II, i, 34)
6. The changeling boy (II, i, 120)

7. Lysander (II, ii, 114. He suggests that Hermia is dark-haired and Helena blonde. He also reveals his capacity for infidelity.)

8. Titania (III, i, 147. She is smitten with Bottom, who is temporarily adorned with an ass's head.)

9. Peaseblossom, Cobweb, Moth, and Mustardseed

10. Puck (III, ii, 115)

11. Hippolyta (IV, i, 117–118. She encapsulates the action and spirit of this play)

12. ". . . because it hath no bottom" (IV, i, 216)

13. Onions and garlic (IV, ii, 42–43)

14. "The lunatic, the lover, and the poet . . ." (V, i, 7)

15. Hippolyta (V, i, 290)

15. Players

1. Richard Burbage
2. Will Kempe
3. Robert Armin
4. David Garrick
5. Sarah Siddons; (*All About Eve*)
6. Edmund Kean
7. William Macready
8. Edwin Booth
9. Henry Irving
10. Ira Aldredge
11. Ellen Terry
12. John Barrymore
13. Laurence Olivier and John Gielgud
14. Orson Welles
15. Paul Scofield

16. *Richard II*

1. Thomas of Woodstock's, Duke of Gloucester
2. "The language I have learnt these forty years . . ." (I, iii, 159)

3. The Irish Wars

4. Herford

5. Salisbury (II, iv, 19–20)

6. Barkloughly

7. "For God's sake let us sit upon the ground
   And tell sad stories of the death of kings . . ." (III, ii, 155–156)

8. ". . . lay the summer's dust with show'rs of blood
   Rain'd from the wounds of slaughtered Englishmen . . ." (III, ii, 43–44)

9. Rue (III, iv, 105)

10. The Bishop of Carlisle (IV, i, 145–147)

11. ". . . a deep well
    That owes two buckets . . ." (IV, i, 184–185)

12. "Was this face the face
    That every day under his household roof
    Did keep ten thousand men?" (IV, i, 281–283);
    similar to V, i, 97 in *Dr. Faustus*

13. Aumerle (V, iii, 131)

14. Pomfret

15. Exton (V, iv, 11)

17. The Playwright and His World

1. 1564

2. Christopher Marlowe

3. Michelangelo; John Calvin

4. John Shakespeare, a tanner and glover; Mary Arden

5. 1582, Anne Hathaway, eight years Shakespeare's senior; Susanna (born 1583), Judith and Hamnet (born 1585, Hamnet died at age 11)

6. 1593, *Venus and Adonis*; 1594, *The Rape of Lucrece*; the Earl of Southhampton

7. Lord Chamberlain's Men; the King's Men

8. 3,000 spectators; 1613

9. 1616; "Second-best bed"

10. "Good friend for Jesus sake forbeare

> To digg the dust encloased heare!
> Bleste be the man that spares these stones
> And curst be he that moves my bones!"

11. 1623; *Pericles*
12. 1642
13. 1558; 1603
14. James VI of Scotland, who became James I of England
15. Guy Fawkes was accused of trying to blow up the House of Lords.
16. Ivan the Terrible
17. 1592
18. Pocahontas
19. Montaigne's *Essais*
20. Galileo

18. Who's Who (III)

1. Alarbus (*Titus Andronicus*)
2. Fleance (*Macbeth*)
3. Sir Eglamour (*The Two Gentlemen of Verona*)
4. Menas (*Antony and Cleopatra*)
5. Francis (*Henry IV, Part 1*)
6. Philostrate (*A Midsummer Night's Dream*)
7. Dr. Pinch (*The Comedy of Errors*)
8. Michael Williams (*Henry V*)
9. Tullus Aufidius (*Coriolanus*)
10. Duchess of Gloucester (*Richard II*)
11. Borachio (*Much Ado About Nothing*)
12. Lady Mortimer (*Henry IV, Part 1*)
13. King John (*King John*)
14. Marina (*Pericles*)
15. Sir Walter Whitmore (*Henry VI, Part 2*)

19. Kings and Such (I)

1. d. (*King Lear*, II, iv, 290–291.
   Goneril callously dismisses her father's pain.)

2. j. (*Henry V*, II, iv, 99–100.

Exeter warns the French king of Henry's military might, subtly shifting blame for potential conflict onto the French themselves.)

3. e. (*Julius Caesar*, II, i, 202–205.

Decius assures his fellow conspirators that Caesar can be persuaded to appear at the Capitol.)

4. h. (*The Winter's Tale*, II, ii, 38–40.

Paulina hopes that a newborn child will cure Leontes of his jealousy.)

5. f. (*Henry IV, Part 1*, III, ii, 4–7.

To his son Hal, King Henry describes his private burden as one who overthrew a king.)

6. g. (*Macbeth*, V, ii, 16–19.

Angus reports that Macbeth is losing control of himself and the citizenry.)

7. i. (*The Tempest*, I, ii, 363–364.

Caliban blames Prospero for bringing civilization to the island.)

8. a. (*Hamlet*, I, iv, 8–9.

Hamlet observes Claudius's revelry as a sign of degeneration in the kingdom.)

9. b. (*Richard III*, IV, ii, 119–120.

Buckingham reveals his shock at Richard's dismissing his request for reward promised earlier.)

10. c. (*Timon of Athens*, IV, iii, 300–301.

Apemantus berates a bitter Timon for his naïveté about human nature.)

20. What's in a Name? (I)

1. Portia: *Julius Caesar, The Merchant of Venice*
2. Brutus: *Julius Caesar, Coriolanus*
3. Sebastian: *Twelfth Night, The Tempest*
4. Bianca: *The Taming of the Shrew, Othello*
5. Margaret: *Henry VI, Parts 1, 2, and 3; Richard III; Much Ado About Nothing*

6. Angelo: *The Comedy of Errors, Measure for Measure*

7. Maria: *Love's Labor's Lost, Twelfth Night*

8. Paris: *Romeo and Juliet, Troilus and Cressida*

9. Claudio: *Much Ado About Nothing, Measure for Measure, Julius Caesar* (Here's where the one sometimes called "Claudius" is found.)

10. Mariana: *All's Well That Ends Well, Measure for Measure*

11. Helena: *A Midsummer Night's Dream, All's Well That Ends Well*

12. Antonio: *The Two Gentlemen of Verona, The Merchant of Venice, Much Ado About Nothing, Twelfth Night, The Tempest*

13. Katherine or Katherina: *The Taming of the Shrew, Love's Labor's Lost, Henry V, Henry VIII*

14. Petruchio: *The Taming of the Shrew, Romeo and Juliet*

15. Buckingham: *Henry VI, Part 2; Richard III; Henry VIII*

16. Pompey: *Measure for Measure, Antony and Cleopatra*

17. Duke of Burgundy: *Henry VI, Part 1; Henry V; King Lear*

18. Ferdinand: *Love's Labor's Lost, The Tempest*

19. Somerset: *Henry VI, Parts 1 and 3*

20. Helen: *Troilus and Cressida, Cymbeline*

21. Colleagues and Rivals

1. l. (1592)
2. e. (c. 1593)
3. i. (c. 1588)
4. h. (c. 1604)
5. g. (1611–1612)
6. m. (1603)
7. a. (1599)
8. j. (c. 1590)
9. d. (c. 1622)
10. n. (c. 1551)
11. b. (c. 1633)
12. f. (1603)
13. k. (1603)
14. o. (c. 1553)
15. c. (c. 1607)

22. Hamlet

1. ". . . the crowing of the cock" (I, i, 157)
2. Cornelius and Voltemand (I, ii, 34)

3. a. ". . . but by no means vulgar" (I, iii, 61).
   b. ". . . but few thy voice" (I, iii, 68).
   c. ". . . but reserve thy judgment" (I, iii, 69).
   d. ". . . to thine own self be true,
   And it must follow, as the night the day,
   Thou canst not then be false to any man" (I, iii, 78–80).
4. Juice of hebona (I, v, 62)
5. "The time is out of joint—O cursed spite,
   That ever I was born to set it right!" (I, v, 188–189)
6. "I doubt it is no other but the main,
   His father's death and our o'erhasty marriage" (II, ii,
56–57).
7. ". . . the play's the thing
   Wherein I'll catch the conscience of the King" (II, ii,
604–605).
8. "Get thee to a nunn'ry . . ." (III, i, 120)
9. Julius Caesar (III, ii, 102)
10. ". . . nephew to the king" (III, ii, 244)
11. Fortinbras (IV, iv, 48)
12. Laertes shouts at Claudius about the death of Polonius
(IV, v, 132–134).
13. ". . . that day our last king Hamlet overcame Fortinbras"
(V, i, 144).
14. "I had my father's signet in my purse,
    Which was the model of that Danish seal" (V, ii, 50).
15. Osric (V, ii, 82)

23. Women

1. f. (*Henry VIII*, IV, ii, 167–170.
   Queen Katherine offers some last words before she is
executed.)
2. i. (*Julius Caesar*, II, i, 299–302.
   Portia tries to convince Brutus that she will not reveal his
plans.)
3. b. (*Othello*, III, ii, 80–83.

Desdemona gently urges her husband to follow her wish that he exonerate Cassio, but she unintentionally begins to rouse his temper.)

4. g. (*King Lear*, III, vii, 5.

Regan orders punishment for the captured Gloucester.)

5. j. (*Macbeth*, I, vii, 49–51.

Lady Macbeth berates her husband for tempting her with the notion that he might murder Duncan and gain the throne.)

6. h. (*Richard III*, I, ii, 43–45.

Lady Anne stands furious over the body of her husband, Prince Edward, then curses the murderer, the Duke of Gloucester, who appears before her.)

7. a. (*Troilus and Cressida*, V, iii, 19–20.

Andromache tries to persuade Hector not to risk individual combat with Achilles.)

8. e. (*As You Like It*, III, ii, 400–402.

Rosalind comforts Orlando, who is unaware that the man whose advice he takes is actually the woman he loves.)

9. c. (*Antony and Cleopatra*, IV, xv, 73–75.

Cleopatra arises from her fainting spell, seemingly changed and determined to prove that her love for Antony is supreme.)

10. d. (*Romeo and Juliet*, III, ii, 90–92.

Juliet chastises the Nurse for wishing evil on Romeo, who has just slain Tybalt.)

24. Scramble

1. Prospero (*The Tempest*)
2. Cicero (*Julius Caesar*)
3. Cassandra (*Troilus and Cressida*)
4. Glendower (*Henry IV, Part 1*)
5. Costard (*Love's Labor's Lost*)
6. Benvolio (*Romeo and Juliet*)
7. Thurio (*The Two Gentlemen of Verona*)

8. Holofernes (*Love's Labor's Lost*)
9. Lepidus (*Antony and Cleopatra*)
10. Donalbain (*Macbeth*)
11. Fortinbras (*Hamlet*)
12. Charmian (*Antony and Cleopatra*)
13. Oberon (*A Midsummer Night's Dream*)
14. Lodovico (*Othello*)
15. Alcibiades (*Timon of Athens*)
16. Trinculo (*The Tempest*)
17. Macmorris (*Henry V*)
18. Pandulph (*King John*)
19. Thaliard (*Pericles*)
20. Cominius (*Coriolanus*)

25. *Henry IV, Parts 1 and 2*

1. Diana (1, I, ii, 25–26)
2. Poins (1, I, ii, 161–166)
3. Mortimer (1, I, iii, 156. Hotspur is married to Mortimer's sister.)
4. Douglas (1, II, iv, 342–343)
5. "I do, I will" (1, II, iv, 480; a response to Falstaff's plea ". . . banish plump Jack, and banish all the world").
6. Glendower (1, III, i, 52)
7. Sir Walter Blunt (1, IV, iii, 40)
8. Vernon (1, V, ii, 66–68)
9. A bottle of sack (1, V, iii, 54)
10. Worcester and Vernon (1, V, v, 14)
11. Morton (2, I, i, 109–111)
12. Falstaff (2, I, ii, 173–174)
13. Officers who intend to arrest Falstaff (2, II, i)
14. Henry, Prince of Wales; John of Lancaster; Humphrey of Gloucester; Thomas of Clarence
15. Ned
16. Pistol, according to Doll Tearsheet (2, II, iv, 72)
17. Feeble (2, III, ii, 156–157)
18. Prince John (2, IV, iii, 89)
19. Henry IV to Hal (2, IV, v, 213–215)

20. "I know thee not old man, fall to thy prayers.
How ill white hairs becomes a fool and jester!" (2, V, v, 47–48)

26. Lovers (I)

1. j. (*A Midsummer Night's Dream*, III, i, 137–139.
Titania is enamored of Bottom, ironically wearing the head of an ass.)
2. g. (*Antony and Cleopatra*, IV, viii, 16–18.
Cleopatra revels in Antony's triumph in combat.)
3. f. (*Romeo and Juliet*, I, v, 92–96.
Moments after Romeo first sees Juliet, he declares devotion to her.)
4. i. (*Richard III*, I, ii, 121–123.
Richard III claims that love for Lady Anne inspired him to murder her husband.)
5. d. (*The Merchant of Venice*, V, i, 54–55.
Lorenzo establishes an atmosphere of romance for Jessica.)
6. h. (*Othello*, II, i, 189–190.
Othello is at his most passionate, unaware that his happiness with Desdemona will be short-lived.)
7. e. (*Much Ado About Nothing*, V, ii, 102–104.
With characteristic wit, Benedick finally reveals his love for Beatrice.)
8. a. (*The Taming of the Shrew*, II, i, 245–246.
Petruchio describes to Katherine the woman he sees within her.)
9. b. (*Hamlet*, V, i, 269–271.
Hamlet rages over the grave of Ophelia.)
10. c. (*The Tempest*, I, ii, 418–420.
Miranda has just caught sight of Ferdinand.)

27. Villains

1. f. (*Much Ado About Nothing*, I, iii, 13–18.
Don John broods on his own misanthropy.)

2. e. (*Richard III*, IV, iv, 297–298.
Richard III offers Queen Elizabeth the possibility of future greatness.)
3. a. (*Titus Andronicus*, II, i, 19–20.
Aaron revels in his plans to gain power.)
4. j. (*Othello*, I, iii, 319–320.
Iago scorns Roderigo's emotions as a manifestation of weakness.)
5. b. (*King Lear*, V, iii, 175.
Edmund realizes that his evil deeds have finally caught up with him.)
6. i. (*Hamlet*, III, iii, 67.
Claudius contemplates his predicament.)
7. d. (*Cymbeline*, I, vi, 126–128.
Iachimo tries to rouse Imogen to revenge against the Queen.)
8. c. (*The Tempest*, II, i, 206–208.
Antonio has not abandoned his ambition to achieve power.)
9. g. (*Henry VI, Part 3*, III, ii, 182–185.
The Duke of Gloucester, soon to become Richard III, revels in his own ability to deceive.)
10. h. (*Measure for Measure*, II, ii, 162–163.
Angelo is taken aback by his own vulnerability to lust.)

28. Clowns and Wits

1. f. (*The Two Gentlemen of Verona*, IV, iv, 9–10.
Launce broods over the lack of trust in his world.)
2. i. (*Hamlet*, V, i, 18–20.
The Gravedigger treats his profession casually, yet also comments indirectly on the themes of action and responsibility.)
3. d. (*King Lear*, I, iv, 160–162.
The Fool reminds Lear of the fatal division of the kingdom for which the King is responsible.)
4. g. (*The Merchant of Venice*, II, ii, 76–77.
Gobbo mocks his blind father but also touches on the division between parent and child that underscores the play.)

5. j. (*As You Like It*, III, ii, 40–43.

Touchstone berates the bewildered Corin with the nasty wit that reveals Touchstone's own emptiness.)

6. a. (*Twelfth Night*, I, v, 5–6.

Feste, perhaps the most melancholy of Shakespeare's clowns, offers his first words.)

7. e. (*Antony and Cleopatra*, V, ii, 260.

In the moments preceding Cleopatra's death, Shakespeare finds opportunity for laughter through this innocent clown who holds a basket of snakes.)

8. b. (*A Midsummer Night's Dream*, III, i, 142–143.

While Bottom accepts Titania's affection with nonchalance, he articulates one of the crucial themes of the play.)

9. h. (*Macbeth*, II, iii, 31–32.

In an amazing interlude after Macbeth has murdered Duncan, the Porter expatiates on the theme of equivocation, a quality that haunts Macbeth now and later.)

10. c. (*Much Ado About Nothing*, IV, ii, 76–78.

Dogberry demands that the insults against him be preserved as evidence.)

29. Words, Words, Words (I)

1. King Lear (*King Lear*)
2. Duke of Gloucester, then Richard III (*Richard III*)
3. Beatrice (*Much Ado About Nothing*)
4. Richard II (*Richard II*)
5. Proteus (*The Two Gentlemen of Verona*)
6. Iago (*Othello*)
7. Prospero (*The Tempest*)
8. Philip the Bastard (*King John*)
9. Portia (*The Merchant of Venice*)
10. Falstaff (*Henry IV, Part 1*)

30. *The Merchant of Venice*

1. ". . . a golden fleece" (I, i, 170)
2. Jacob and Laban (I, iii, 71–90)

3. Jessica to Launcelot Gobbo (II, iii, 2–3)

4. "What gold and jewels she is furnish'd with . . ." (II, iv, 31)

5. The Prince of Morocco (II, vii)

6. The Prince of Arragon (II, ix)

7. Rialto (III, i, 1)

8. "Why, revenge" (III, i, 71)

9. A ring (III, i, 118–123)

10. Her cousin's, Doctor Bellario (III, iv, 50)

11. Antonio in court (IV, i, 114–115. He seems almost eager to die.)

12. "He presently become a Christian;

The other, that he do record a gift,

Here in the court, of all he dies possess'd

Upon his son Lorenzo and his daughter" (IV, i, 387–390).

13. Lorenzo (V, i, 83–85)

14. "So shines a good deed in a naughty world" (V, i, 90–91).

15. Gratiano

31. Battles

1. i. (Joan of Pucelle's triumph)

2. a. (accepted as the start of the War of the Roses)

3. e. (where Brutus dies, as Caesar's ghost warned)

4. g. (where Richard III dies, shouting with ironic anger, "A horse, a horse! my kingdom for a horse" [V, v, 1])

5. h. (where John of Lancaster tricks the rebel troops into surrendering)

6. j. (the apex of Henry V's career)

7. d. (the victory of the Yorks, the downfall of Margaret, and the death of her son, Prince Edward, at the hands of the three sons of York)

8. c. (the downfall of Antony)

9. b. (where King John defeats the French and captures Arthur, his rival for the throne)

10. f. (where Hotspur dies, slain by Hal, although Falstaff later claims credit)

32. Honor

1. h. (*Antony and Cleopatra*, III, iv, 22–24.
Antony explains to Octavia the necessity of his military exploits.)
   2. i. (*Coriolanus*, V, iii, 149–150.
Volumnia tries to bully her son, Coriolanus, into refraining from war against their native city, Rome.)
   3. b. (*Henry IV, Part 2*, II, iii, 7–8.
Northumberland justifies his participation in a conflict he will soon evade.)
   4. g. (*Henry IV, Part 1*, I, iii, 201–202.
Hotspur boasts to his fellow conspirators but also demonstrates his own mad romantic streak.)
   5. c. (*Julius Caesar*, I, ii, 88–89.
Brutus tries to sound noble but simultaneously reveals his point of weakness.)
   6. j. (*Othello*, V, ii, 294–295.
After murdering Desdemona, Othello tries to exonerate himself.)
   7. d. (*Hamlet*, IV, iv, 53–56.
Hamlet looks to Fortinbras to inspire himself to revenge.)
   8. a. (*Henry V*, IV, iii, 28–29.
The King rouses his "band of brothers" to the grandeur of military glory.)
   9. f. (*Troilus and Cressida*, V, iii, 26–28.
Hector accepts the challenge by Achilles, a combat that, as Hector knows, will likely leave Hector dead.)
   10. e. (*Henry IV, Part 1*, V, i, 131–134.
Falstaff reflects on military glory. In the play he responds most directly to Hotspur, quoted above, but this speech stands in opposition to all the figures throughout Shakespeare's plays who base their actions on the uncertain rewards of honor.)

33. Criticism

1. Maurice Morgann
2. William Hazlitt

3. Thomas De Quincey

4. A. C. Bradley

5. Harley Granville-Barker

6. G. Wilson Knight

7. Caroline Spurgeon

8. J. Dover Wilson

9. Mark Van Doren

10. E. M. Tillyard

11. Ernest Jones

12. Harold Goddard

13. F. R. Leavis

14. Jan Kott

15. Victor L. Cahn (Hey, who's asking these questions?)

34. Words, Words, Words (II)

1. Hermia (*A Midsummer Night's Dream*)

2. Gloucester (*King Lear*)

3. Wolsey (*Henry VIII*)

4. Isabella (*Measure for Measure*)

5. Bertram (*All's Well That Ends Well*)

6. Enobarbus (*Antony and Cleopatra*)

7. Ophelia (*Hamlet*)

8. Henry V (*Henry V*)

9. Margaret (*Henry VI, Part 3*)

10. Sebastian (*Twelfth Night*)

35. A Matter of Identity

1. Rosaline is the object of Romeo's love before he sets eyes on Juliet (I, i).

2. Leah was Shylock's wife (III, i, 121).

3. Sycorax was Caliban's mother (I, ii, 331).

4. Susan was the Nurse's daughter (I, iii, 18–19).

5. Antonio was Petruchio's father (I, ii, 54).

6. Gerard de Narbon was Helena's father (I, i, 27).

7. Richard the Lionhearted was the father of Faulconbridge, the Bastard (I, i, 50).

8. Macdonwald was defeated by Macbeth in battle (I, i, 9–23).

9. Sir Rowland de Boys was the father of Oliver and Orlando (I, ii, 222).

10. Lord Scales and Lord Hungerford are taken prisoners by the French (I, i, 148).

All are mentioned but never appear onstage.

36. *Henry V*

1. The Scots (I, ii, 136–138)
2. Salic Law
3. Tennis balls (I, ii, 257)
4. Falstaff (II, iii)
5. Earl of Cambridge, Lord Scroop, and Sir Thomas Grey
6. Pistol (II, iii, 55–56; providing a less romantic view of battle)
7. Nym (II, iii)
8. Bardolph, one of the King's cronies from his time in the tavern, steals a pax from a church (III, vi, 40). Henry's sentence (III, vi, 107–110) recalls Falstaff's warning (*Henry IV, Part 1*, I, ii, 62).
9. Boy (IV, iv, 69)
10. Aumerle (in *Richard II*)
11. St. Crispian's Day
12. 10,000 (IV, viii, 87)
13. Twenty-five (IV, viii, 106)
14. Pistol; Fluellen (V, i, 46–47)
15. She dies "i' the spittle/Of a malady of France" (V, i, 81–82). The "malady" in question is venereal disease.

37. Shakespeare and Film

1. *The Taming of the Shrew*
2. Max Reinhardt directed.
   Mickey Rooney played Puck.
   James Cagney played Bottom.

Dick Powell played Lysander.

Joe E. Brown played Flute.

Olivia de Havilland played Hermia.

3. George Cukor directed.

Norma Shearer and Leslie Howard played Juliet and Romeo.

John Barrymore played Mercutio.

4. Elizabeth Bergner

5. Jack Benny

6. Robert Newton

7. *A Double Life*

8. William Walton

9. Marlon Brando played Antony.

James Mason played Brutus.

John Gielgud played Cassius.

Louis Calhern played Caesar.

Greer Garson played Calphurnia.

Deborah Kerr played Portia.

Edmund O'Brien played Casca.

Joseph L. Mankiewicz directed.

10. *Joe Macbeth*

11. Laurence Olivier played Richard III.

John Gielgud played Clarence.

Ralph Richardson played Buckingham.

Olivier directed.

12. *The Tempest*

13. *Chimes at Midnight* ("We have heard the chimes at midnight, Master Shallow." *Henry IV, Part 2*, III, ii, 215)

14. Peter Brook

15. Roman Polanski

16. Vincent Price; Diana Rigg

17. Paul Mazursky

18. *King Lear*; Akira Kurosawa

19. Peter Greenaway

20. Tom Stoppard, the playwright

21. Ronald Harwood wrote the play.

Albert Finney played Sir.

Tom Courtney played the dresser.

22. *Hamlet*, directed by Kenneth Branagh
23. Anthony Hopkins
24. Al Pacino
25. Leonardo DiCaprio and Claire Danes
26. *My Own Private Idaho*
27. *The Taming of the Shrew*
28. *King Lear*
29. *Love's Labour's Lost*
30. *She's the Man*

38. Lovers (II)

1. i. (*Henry V*, V, ii, 165–166.

Henry V, ever blunt, yet political, declares his affections for Katherine of France.)

2. c. (*The Winter's Tale*, IV, iv, 41–43.

Florizel assures Perdita that his love can overcome all social barriers.)

3. j. (*Coriolanus*, II, i, 175–177.

In a respite from his customary military posture, Coriolanus comforts his demure wife, Virgilia.)

4. h. (*Henry VI, Part 2*, III, ii, 362–364.

The ruthless Suffolk becomes surprisingly tender when he must part from the even more ruthless Queen Margaret.)

5. f. (*Troilus and Cressida*, III, ii, 126–129.

Before she departs for the Greek side as part of a bargain, Cressida comforts Troilus in her own unique manner.)

6. g. (*The Comedy of Errors*, II, ii, 181–182.

Antipholus of Syracuse is happily confused by Adriana's affection for the man she mistakes for her husband.)

7. e. (*A Midsummer Night's Dream*, II, ii, 115–116.

Under the influence of Puck's magic, Lysander proclaims the power of reason as he helplessly switches his infatuation from Hermia to Helena.)

8. a. (*Love's Labor's Lost*, V, ii, 837–840.

The formerly cynical Berowne offers to perform for Rosaline a service appropriate to a traditional Renaissance lover.)

9. b. (*All's Well That Ends Well*, I, i, 85–87.

Helena pines, somewhat inexplicably, for the insufferable Bertram, who is several social stations higher than she.)

10. d. (*King Lear*, V, i, 6–9.

Regan throws herself at Edmund, as desperate to have him for herself as to keep him from Goneril.)

39. Potpourri: The Comedies

1. ". . . there shall be no more cakes and ale?" (*Twelfth Night*, II, iii, 114–116)

2. Dromio (*The Comedy of Errors*, IV, ii, 58)

3. Sir Eglamour (*The Two Gentlemen of Verona*)

4. Slender, Caius, and Fenton

5. Mistress Quickly

6. ". . . some achieve greatness, and some have greatness thrust upon 'em." Malvolio (*Twelfth Night*, II, v, 144–146. These lines are later echoed by Feste [V, i, 370–372].)

7. Benedick (*Much Ado About Nothing*, V, ii, 40–41)

8. "The infant," "the whining schoolboy," "the lover," "a soldier," "the justice," "the lean and slipper'd pantaloon," and "second childishness" (*As You Like It*, II, vii, 139–166)

9. Sir Topas the curate (*Twelfth Night*, IV, ii)

10. A chain (*The Comedy of Errors*, III, ii)

11. Maria

12. Duke Senior (*As You Like It*, II, i, 3–4)

13. Holofernes (*Love's Labor's Lost*, V, ii)

14. Falstaff (*The Merry Wives of Windsor*, V, v)

15. Viola (*Twelfth Night*, III, iv, 375)

16. The names of two houses in *The Comedy of Errors*. The Phoenix marks the home of Antipholus of Ephesus, and the Porpentine marks the house of the Courtezan.

17. Beatrice (*Much Ado About Nothing*, III, i, 107–108)

18. Silvius (*As You Like It*)

19. Olivia to Malvolio (*Twelfth Night*, I, v, 90)

20. Crab (*The Two Gentlemen of Verona*)

40. *Macbeth*

1. Although they look like women, they have beards (I, ii, 45–47).

2. The Thane of Cawdor (I, iv, 7–8)

3. Prince of Cumberland (I, iv, 39)

4. ". . . o' th' milk of human kindness . . ." (I, v, 16–17)

5. "Had he not resembled
My father as he slept, I had done 't" (II, ii, 12–13).

6. "Amen" (II, ii, 26)

7. Macduff (II, iii)

8. Scone

9. ". . . the perfect spy o' th' time . . ." (III, i, 129)

10. In Macbeth's chair

11. Sleep (III, iv, 140)

12. "Something wicked this way comes" (IV, i, 45)

13. Whether Banquo's children will be kings (IV, i, 102–103)

14. An armed head, a bloody child, and a child crowned, with a tree in his hand.

15. Young Siward (V, vii)

41. Supporting Players

1. s. (*Timon of Athens*)

2. p. (*Romeo and Juliet*)

3. h. (*The Merchant of Venice*)

4. j. (*As You Like It*)

5. k. (*Hamlet*)

6. a. (*The Comedy of Errors*)

7. t. (*The Merchant of Venice*)

8. q. (*Twelfth Night*)

9. m. (*All's Well That Ends Well*)

10. e. (*Henry IV, Part 2*)
11. d. (*Romeo and Juliet*)
12. r. (*The Two Gentlemen of Verona*)
13. f. (*The Merry Wives of Windsor*)
14. c. (*Much Ado About Nothing*)
15. b. (*Julius Caesar*)
16. l. (*Love's Labor's Lost*)
17. g. (*Troilus and Cressida*)
18. n. (*The Two Gentlemen of Verona*)
19. o. (*Twelfth Night*)
20. i. (*Cymbeline*)

42. Soliloquies (II)

1. i. (*Much Ado About Nothing*, II, iii, 28–30.
   Benedick resists his attraction to Beatrice.)
2. h. (*Coriolanus*, IV, iv, 12–13.
   Coriolanus bitterly reflects on the treachery of his fellow citizens.)
3. f. (*Henry VI, Part 3*, II, v, 19–20.
   Henry VI laments his royal responsibilities.)
4. j. (*Timon of Athens*, IV, i, 3–6.
   Timon urges the onset of chaos.)
5. c. (*Troilus and Cressida*, I, ii, 286–287.
   Cressida muses on the singular power of women.)
6. g. (*Othello*, II, i, 291–293.
   Iago rationalizes his feelings for Othello and Desdemona.)
7. b. (*The Winter's Tale*, IV, iv, 670–672.
   Autolycus reflects on the techniques of his profession.)
8. e. (*All's Well That Ends Well*, IV, ii, 71–73.
   Diana weighs her alternatives with Bertram.)
9. a. (*Julius Caesar*, II, i, 15–17.
   Brutus ponders action against Caesar.)
10. d. (*Love's Labor's Lost*, III, i, 174–178.
    Berowne is flabbergasted at his vulnerability to the charms of Rosaline.)

43. Sources

1. g.	5. j.	9. d.
2. i.	6. b.	10. e.
3. a.	7. f.	11. l.
4. k.	8. c.	12. h.

44. Potpourri: The First Tetralogy

1. The Duke of Suffolk
2. Joan of Pucelle (*Henry VI, Part 1*, I, ii, 113–114)
3. Lady Bona
4. *Henry VI, Part 2* (IV, ii, 76); Dick the Butcher
5. Margaret
6. Earl of Derby
7. Eleven, all of characters whom we have seen as victims of the King's plotting:

 Young Prince Edward
 Henry VI
 Clarence
 Rivers, Grey, and Vaughan
 Two young Princes
 Hastings
 Lady Anne
 Buckingham

8. Talbot is so scorned by the Countess of Auvergne (*Henry VI, Part 1*, II, iii, 22).
9. The three surviving sons of York (King Edward, Clarence, and Richard, all of whom stab him [*Henry VI, Part 3*, V, v, 38–42])
10. Simpox (*Henry VI, Part 2*, II, i)
11. Jack Cade (*Henry VI, Part 2*, III, i, 356)
12. Joan of Pucelle dismisses the treacherous Burgundy (*Henry VI, Part 1*, III, iii, 85).
13. These words are the first uttered by Richard, son of York, soon to be Duke of Gloucester, eventually to be Richard III.
14. The second murderer remembers his potential reward once Clarence has been killed (*Richard III*, I, iv, 125).

15. Three suns (*Henry VI, Part 3*, II, i, 26)

16. Richard III orders Catesby to bring back the crowd (*Richard III*, III, vii, 224).

17. Alexander Iden says these words after he has slain Jack Cade (*Henry VI, Part 2*, IV, x, 77–79).

18. Henry VI (*Henry VI, Part 1*, III, i, 72–73)

19. Jane Shore (*Richard III*, III, iv, 67–72)

20. Richard, Duke of York, explains that his mother, Anne Mortimer, the sister of Edmund Mortimer, married Richard, Earl of Cambridge. Mortimer, named by Richard II as heir apparent, was descended from Clarence, third son of Edward III. Henry VI was descended from the fourth son, John of Gaunt. Thus by order of the laws of succession, York argues that the throne belongs to him. Such is the matter that York insists is "plain."

45. Brothers and Sisters

1. o. (*Henry IV, Part 1*)
2. q. (*The Comedy of Errors*)
3. r. (*Henry VI, Part 3*)
4. s. (*Twelfth Night*)
5. d. (*Troilus and Cressida*)
6. i. (*As You Like It*)
7. l. (*The Tempest*)
8. c. (*Measure for Measure*)
9. m. (*Henry VI, Parts 1 and 2*)
10. b. (*Henry VI, Part 3*)
11. k. (*Much Ado About Nothing*)
12. h. (*Titus Andronicus*)
13. e. (*Henry IV, Parts 1 and 2*)
14. a. (*Henry IV, Part 2*)
15. f. (*Titus Andronicus*)
16. t. (*Richard III*)
17. p. (*Hamlet*)
18. n. (*Macbeth*)
19. j. (*Cymbeline*)
20. g. (*Much Ado About Nothing*)

46. Kings and Such (II)

1. g. (*Henry VIII*, II, i, 90–92.
The condemned Buckingham affirms his loyalty to King Henry VIII.)

2. a. (*Henry VI, Part 3*, III, ii, 125–127.
The Duke of Gloucester plots the downfall of his brother, Edward IV.)

3. j. (*Measure for Measure*, III, ii, 117–119.
An unsuspecting Lucio comments about Duke Vincentio, disguised before Lucio as a Friar.)

4. c. (*Richard II*, III, iii, 68–71.
York offers tribute to Richard II's grandeur, while unintentionally affirming that the King is playing the role of ruler.)

5. h. (*Antony and Cleopatra*, I, iii, 66–68.
After accepting the death of Fulvia, his wife, with equanimity, Antony reassures Cleopatra of his devotion.)

6. d. (*Henry VI, Part 1*, V, v, 67–69.
Suffolk convinces Henry that the King's stature is such that he need not marry wealth and power and that Margaret's royal birth is sufficient to make her a worthy match.)

7. b. (*Pericles*, I, i, 91–93.
Pericles, realizing that the answer to the puzzle posed by King Antiochus is "incest" and that the king himself is guilty of the crime, refrains from answering.)

8. e. (*Henry IV, Part 2*, IV, v, 138–140.
King Henry IV is reassured by his son Hal, who explains that he took the crown only because he thought his father to be dead.)

9. f. (*Henry VI, Part 3*, I, i, 216–217.
Margaret lambastes her husband, Henry VI, for giving succession to the throne to the Duke of York.)

10. i. (*King John*, V, i, 17–18, 24.
Pandulph tries to persuade the vacillating King John to capitulate before the Pope.)

47. The Roman Tragedies

1. Brutus, Cassius, Casca, Trebonius, Caius Ligarius, Decius Brutus, Metellus Cimber, Cinna
2. ". . . the northern star" (III, i, 60)
3. Bassianus (*Titus Andronicus*, II, iii, 226)
4. A gilded butterfly (*Coriolanus*, I, iii, 60)
5. Octavius Caesar (*Antony and Cleopatra*, IV, vi, 4)
6. ". . . th' rock Tarpeian" (III, i, 212)
7. She swallows fire (*Julius Caesar*, IV, iii, 156)
8. Brutus to Cassius (*Julius Caesar*, IV, iii, 37)
9. ". . . for pulling scarfs off Caesar's images . . ." (*Julius Caesar*, I, ii, 285–286)
10. Agrippa; Octavia's (*Antony and Cleopatra*, II, ii, 134–136)
11. Coriolanus disdains displaying his wounds for the populace (II, ii, 144–146).
12. "Cowards die many times before their deaths,
    The valiant never taste of death but once." (*Julius Caesar*, II, ii, 32–33)
13. One: Lucius
14. Strato (*Julius Caesar*, V, v, 51)
15. Enobarbus (*Antony and Cleopatra*, II, vi, 126)
16. Menenius (*Coriolanus*, I, i, 95–155)
17. Marcus (*Titus Andronicus*, III, ii, 51)
18. "Twelve several times." (*Coriolanus*, IV, v, 122)
19. Proculeius (*Antony and Cleopatra*, IV, xv, 48)
20. Octavius speaks to Antony in anticipation of their future strife (*Julius Caesar*, V, i, 20).

48. Words, Words, Words (III)

1. *Othello*
    (The speakers are Othello, Iago, Emilia, and Desdemona.)
2. *Troilus and Cressida*
    (The speakers are Ulysses, Troilus, Ajax, and Thersites.)

3. *Henry IV, Part 2*
(The speakers are Falstaff, Henry IV, Prince John, and Prince Hal.)
4. *As You Like It*
(The speakers are the Duke, Jaques, Orlando, Rosalind.)
5. *King Lear*
(The speakers are Edgar, Edmund, Kent, and Cordelia.)
6. *King John*
(The speakers are the Bastard, King John, Lewis, and Pandulph.)
7. *Julius Caesar*
(The speakers are Casca, Cassius, the First Plebeian, and Antony.)
8. *Cymbeline*
(The speakers are Jachimo, Cloten, Imogen, and Cymbeline.)
9. *Macbeth*
(The speakers are Duncan, Lady Macbeth, Macduff, and Macbeth.)
10. *The Winter's Tale*
(The speakers are Leontes, Paulina, Polixenes, and Hermione.)

49. What's in a Name? (II)

1. *Richard II, Macbeth*
2. *The Merchant of Venice, The Tempest*
3. *Hamlet, Cymbeline*
4. *Titus Andronicus, A Midsummer Night's Dream, Antony and Cleopatra*
5. *Antony and Cleopatra, Timon of Athens*
6. *Troilus and Cressida, Antony and Cleopatra*
7. *The Taming of the Shrew, Measure for Measure*
8. *Julius Caesar, Timon of Athens*
9. *The Comedy of Errors, Romeo and Juliet, The Merchant of Venice, Much Ado About Nothing*

10. *Titus Andronicus, The Two Gentlemen of Verona, Twelfth Night*

11. *Hamlet, The Tempest*

12. *The Comedy of Errors, Othello, The Winter's Tale* (Emilia is also the name of a character in *The Two Noble Kinsmen*, the last dramatic work to which Shakespeare contributed.)

13. *Julius Caesar, Timon of Athens*

14. *Coriolanus, The Tempest*

15. *Titus Andronicus, Julius Caesar, Cymbeline, Timon of Athens*

50. Songs

1. e. (*Love's Labor's Lost*, V, ii, 901–902.

Armado muses on the moods of married men, trivial against the passage of time.)

2. f. (*The Merchant of Venice*, III, ii, 63–64.

Portia and her musicians sing while Bassanio reflects on the caskets of gold, silver, and lead. Do the lyrics, all of which end in "-ed," hint at "lead," the proper choice?)

3. h. (*The Tempest*, I, ii, 397–403.

Ariel persuades Ferdinand that his father, Alonso, King of Naples, has drowned.)

4. j. (*As You Like It*, II, vii, 174–176.

Amiens reaffirms the theme of jealousy that pervades the play.)

5. a. (*The Two Gentlemen of Verona*, IV, ii, 39–43.

At Thurio's request, musicians serenade his love, while an angry Proteus and a jealous Julia stand to the side.)

6. c. (*Much Ado About Nothing*, II, iii, 62–65.

Balthazar warns women about the weakness of men's vows, a reflection in particular of Claudio.)

7. i. (*Hamlet*, IV, v, 23–26.

Ophelia, left mad by her father's death, broods on lost love.)

8. b. (*Romeo and Juliet*, II, iv, 134–139.

Mercutio offers the Nurse some bawdy lyrics that appeal to both of them.)

9. d. (*Henry IV, Part 2*, V, iii, 17–22.
Justice Silence exudes a spirit of bonhomie.)
10. g. (*Cymbeline*, IV, ii, 258–261.
Guiderius generously mourns Cloten, their enemy, but also their brother.)

51. Death Scenes

1. j. (*Troilus and Cressida*)
2. d. (*Measure for Measure*)
3. i. (*King Lear*)
4. g. (*The Winter's Tale*)
5. a. (*Richard III*)
6. h. (*King John*)
7. c. (*Hamlet*)
8. e. (*Julius Caesar*)
9. b. (*Titus Andronicus*)
10. f. (*Henry VI, Part 1*)

52. Closing Lines

1. e. Richmond, the future Henry VII, announces the end of the War of the Roses.

2. j. Benedick puts aside the question of Don John's fate, then joins the dance, both literal and metaphoric, that he has so long resisted.

3. i. Edgar comments with resignation on the enormity of Lear's tragedy.

4. h. Pandarus makes a last appeal to those of his trade, encapsulating the play's thematic uniting of sexuality and warfare.

5. b. Henry IV anticipates a trip to offer penance for his crimes against Richard II, a voyage the new King will never take.

6. d. Feste reflects on the brevity of the individual human life in contrast to the great pageant of time. In *King Lear*, the Fool sings similar lines (III, ii, 74–77).

7. c. In a singular, yet apt, gesture, Rosalind, a woman, is allowed to close the play that she has dominated.

8. f. Philip the Bastard unites his countrymen with his customary nationalistic fervor.

9. a. Fortinbras orders a military tribute for that most unmilitary of heroes, Hamlet.

10. g. Prospero bids farewell to the audience and his art, words that many have taken to be part of Shakespeare's own valedictory.

ABOUT THE AUTHOR

Victor L. Cahn is professor of English at Skidmore College, where he teaches courses in Shakespeare, modern drama, and the history of drama. He has written three other books on Shakespeare, including *Shakespeare the Playwright: A Companion to the Complete Tragedies, Histories, Comedies, and Romances*, named an Outstanding Academic Book by *Choice*. His other works include critical volumes on Tom Stoppard and Harold Pinter; *Conquering College: A Guide for Undergraduates*; the memoir *Classroom Virtuoso*; and the novel *Romantic Trapezoid*. His articles and reviews have appeared in such varied publications as *Modern Drama, The Literary Review, The Chronicle of Higher Education, The New York Times,* and *Variety.*

He is the author of numerous plays, several of which have been produced Off-Broadway and regionally: *Embraceable Me, Roses in December, Fit to Kill* (all published by Samuel French), *Sheepskin/Bottom of the Ninth,* and the one-man show *Sherlock Solo,* which he has performed. He has also taken leading roles in plays by Shakespeare, Pinter, Simon, Coward, Gurney, and Knott.